There is an eternal battle going on around all of us, a battle for our souls. How is this battle fought? Where is there safety?

Author and pastor J. Hamilton Weston believes this battle is crucial and that we need to know what is going on and what God has provided for our protection in this battle. Looking at scripture, Weston discusses the nature of the conflict, who are our enemies, and then takes on what we have on our side in this conflict: God's armor, God's protection, God's promises, and yes, God's rewards.

You can't avoid this conflict. It's happening around you. But you can be victorious. This book will help guide you to the right path.

The Battle for Eternity

The War for Souls, Circa: Now

J. Hamilton Weston

Energion Publications
Gonzalez, Florida
2020

Copyright © 2020, J. Hamilton Weston

Scripture taken from the New King James Version®. Copyright © 1982 by Thomas Nelson. Used by permission. All rights reserved.

ISBN: 978-1-63199-061-8
eISBN: 978-1-63199-063-2
Library of Congress Control Number: 2020938970

Energion Publications
P. O. Box 841
Gonzalez, FL 32560

energion.com

Acknowledgements

In writing this book on Spiritual Warfare, I am continually in prayer for all the spiritual troops as they are in harm's way every moment of every day. I am dedicating this book to my son, who is in the United States Marine Corps, those who serve with him, and to all branches of the military. When they are deployed, they fight for our freedom and the freedom of those who cannot fight for themselves, domestically and abroad. And more than anything in this world I give the Father, Son, and Holy Spirit all the praise, honor, and glory. In Jesus' Most Precious Name, Amen!

TABLE OF CONTENTS

Acknowledgements iii
Introduction vii

1 The Invincible Obedient 1
2 The Conflict 15
3 The Enemies of Your Soul 43
4 Our Weapons 65
5 The Armor of God 75
6 Our Divine Protector 87
7 Our Divine Protection 97
8 The Promises 105
9 The Rewards 121
10 VICTORY! 135

Conclusion 143

Introduction

> *In the beginning was the Word, and the Word was with God, and the Word was God. He was in the beginning with God. All things were made through Him, and without Him nothing was made that was made. In Him was life, and the life was the light of men. And the light shines in the darkness, and the darkness did not comprehend it.* **(John 1:1-5)**

The study of God and His relationship to His creation has been a concern producing great debate since the beginning. As the Apostle John opens his version of the gospel of Jesus Christ the Son of God, he paints the picture of Jesus the Christ, the Holy Son of God, and His divine relationship to the Father. It was difficult considering how to introduce this study on the spiritual battle we face daily. But, we must first be willing to go back to where the story begins and with whom it begins. Why do you think Jesus had to die for you and me? He could have accomplished His victory over evil a thousand other ways, right? As this subject begins to unfold, we will begin to see that there was much more to the story and more overall individuals involved in our battle for eternal life.

What better place to start than at the beginning. In the gospel according to John the Apostle, beginning in chapter one and verse one, he establishes several things that truly set Jesus apart from any other person born from woman. The vivid description in the first five verses are statements none of which are simple for us to understand. But, to fully comprehend the reach of God's mercy and grace we must first understand the sacrifice He made for us.

The opening verses, like I said, are very vivid descriptions of God in action and Word.

THE WORD OF GOD

The vision we have when we read "In the beginning was the Word, and the Word was with God and the Word was God" is a sense of completeness. The question is "What is the Word and what was it doing at creation?" The place to begin, ironically enough, is at the beginning.

> ***In the beginning God created the heavens and the earth. The earth was without form, and void; and darkness was on the face of the deep. And the Spirit of God was hovering over the face of the waters. (Genesis 1:1-2)***

In the first two verses of Genesis, the writer gives us the initial vision of God's creation process. He "created" the foundations for everything to sustain life for His new creation, both on earth and the heavens. When God prepared the earth and heavens for His creation, He created it for the refuge of life to grow apart from the battle raging as light and darkness, good and evil fought for reign. But, God created a good and perfect earth and heaven. As He formed the earth, the Spirit of God hovered over the waters.

God the Father initially created the heavens and earth. Then, God the Holy Spirit hovered over the waters and blessed the creation and prepared it for the establishment of life. As darkness was on the face of the deep, the Spirit of God passed by and brought light into an otherwise pure dark portion of creation. The earth was without form and void because God was molding the heavens and earth into His vision.

THE LIGHT OF THE WORLD

> ***Then God said, "Let there be light"; and there was light. And God saw the light, that it was good; and God divided***

the light from the darkness. God called the light Day, and the darkness He called Night. So the evening and the morning were the first day. **(Genesis 1:3-5)**

The word then entered the picture when God spoke. The first words spoken by God the Father was "Let there be Light." What do these words have to do with the battle for eternity? Everything! Because when God spoke these words, then light was introduced into the otherwise darkness. The first that one notices that when God spoke, the Word, the Son of God, had entered the picture of creation. Jesus said to His disciples in the gospel of John chapter eight verse twelve, **"I am the light of the world. He who follows Me shall not walk in darkness, but have the light of life."** Understanding Jesus as the light of the world can help us better see the meaning behind the belief of Jesus as the light that entered the darkness at creation and overtook it by the word of God. The battle began with the creation and introduction of light into an otherwise dark and formless earth and heaven. The first time Jesus was introduced into the big picture of God plan was at creation and there was opposition in the heavens from that point.

The focus of this study is to attempt to better understand the eternal battle that is raging around everyone every day. The concern for me as a pastor is that my church and those who we are in contact with are looking to Jesus Christ for strength and not leaning on me, the pastor or shepherd, for all their strength and focus. This is because I am but a human like all others and I have faults and I am a sinner saved by the grace of God as they are in their lives. When we focus on all things spiritual, then there is a tendency to forget the mission set before us by our Lord and Savior Jesus Christ. But, if we focus on the physical, we then tend to forget the fact that Jesus has sent the Holy Spirit to be our defender and strength in all things good and bad that effect our daily life.

As we grow in our relationship with Jesus through the power and guidance of the Holy Spirit, we become stronger the more we lean on Him. The battle not only is outside of us but also rests within us as well as in our reaction to sin. We can blame our misfortune on Satan or say that the devil made me do it, but the truth of the matter is that we have free will and we are created by God the Father to make our own choices. The problem is that we are only calling on Christ to help us in the tough times and we want immediate action. God's timing is not our timing. Jesus has told us in His word that we need to be strong and very courageous. Are we standing firm in our faith? Do we truly believe that the same Spirit of God that hovered over the waters of the deep and brought light to stand against darkness cannot stand strong with you and me through the battles of life? We do not battle against flesh and blood, even though we see evil all around us. We are warned in scripture concerning this whole concept. Jesus said to His disciples,

> ***And Jesus answered and said to them: "Take heed that no one deceives you. For many will come in My name, saying, 'I am the Christ,' and will deceive many. And you will hear of wars and rumors of wars. See that you are not troubled; for all these things must come to pass, but the end is not yet. For nation will rise against nation, and kingdom against kingdom. And there will be famines, pestilences, and earthquakes in various places. All these are the beginning of sorrows." (Matthew 24:4-8)***

The battles that rage in the heavens are also raging on earth. The earthquakes, great natural disasters, such the most powerful hurricanes, famines, and pestilences are all spoken of in scripture. The end times are nearer now than ever before. The greatest threat has always been in the people of God themselves. The battles in the spiritual realm are real. In Matthew, Jesus is telling His disciples that you must be ready to stand firm always, not only in the times that you can visually witness. He tells them that these signs will only be the beginning. How the Christian chooses to respond to those demanding situations is what determines the true reflection and power of Christ in the life of the believer.

In the passages in Matthew, Jesus is teaching His disciples about preparedness and readiness for the coming end times. I believe that all that occurs on earth is occurring in the heavens. The wars and rumors of wars and devastation is occurring in the spiritual realm. The battle is for the souls of humanity. It will not end until one has destroyed the other. The beauty of the story is that the ending has already been determined by God the Father. The Son will make the final strike and the forces of evil will be destroyed. We have read the end of the book. It is truth and we as Christians who believe it, should live in that hope.

Our Mighty Commander of the Heavenly Hosts

> *Now I saw heaven opened, and behold, a white horse. And He who sat on him was called Faithful and True, and in righteousness He judges and makes war. His eyes were like a flame of fire, and on His head were many crowns. He had a name written that no one knew except Himself. He was clothed with a robe dipped in blood, and His name is called The Word of God.* **(Revelation 19:11-13)**

In whom does your hope rest? When you read this chapter from the Book of Revelation to the Apostle John, what do you see? As powerful as Satan may be in his own right, there is no comparison to the power and glory of the Son of God. Notice the language in these verses. The Son of God will not direct the host from His throne in heaven. He will lead the charge against the dragon and his armies. He will defeat him and the evil that follows after him. We, as believers of Jesus Christ and who follow His commands, must be prepared to fight and stand the ground for the sake of the gospel of Jesus Christ. In verse eleven of chapter nine, the Son of God, the one riding on the white horse, judges and makes war in righteousness. The devil cannot stand against the pure righteousness of God in His Son. Our hope is in the mighty Son of God!

Close your eyes and visualize the picture being painted for you. The earth is trembling with great excitement and anticipation. You look and are awe struck by the sight of the sky opening beyond a clear day to see the heavens open with a great white light and the sound of the trumpets of heaven sounding. The only thing on your mind is to fall on your face because you are not sure what is happening. You strain to look up to the sky to the white horse riding from the heavens and your spirit reacts to the sight of the one who is sitting on the horse. He is glory, Truth, and Faithfulness in its purest form. Countless white horses and those riding are clothed in white robes, so white it is indescribable. You suddenly realize your unworthiness to witness such an amazing sight. The One on the white horse leading the charge has eyes of flames and His robe is dipped in blood. His name is called the Word of God!

What a glorious picture our minds should display. Then, why do we not live with that visual before us? Do we truly realize that Jesus is the Son of God and is ready with the hosts of heaven to defeat Satan whenever God the Father gives the Word?

The focus of this study is to make awareness of the spiritual war that is taking place around you. Also, the study should prayerfully have you to stand strong and be very courageous in your faith because our deliverance draws very near. Many people, even the elite Christians, are oblivious of the spiritual war raging around every moment of every day. The spiritual realm does not sleep or take vacations or even breaks, but it is a continuous war that is raging for the souls of humanity. God created Man in His own image, but Free Will is the Gift of God that was used against first of His creation and it is that gift is bringing its salvation. Read this prayerfully and search the scriptures diligently for yourself and know that the Word is Truth.

> *And I saw the beast, the kings of the earth, and their armies, gathered together to make war against Him who sat on the horse and against His army. Then the beast was captured, and with him the false prophet who worked signs*

> *in his presence, by which he deceived those who received the mark of the beast and those who worshiped his image. These two were cast alive into the lake of fire burning with brimstone. And the rest were killed with the sword which proceeded from the mouth of Him who sat on the horse. And all the birds were filled with their flesh.* **(Revelation 19:19-21)**

The defeat of the armies of the Satan is already complete, it just must play out in time. So, when you read the end of the book of Revelation there is a sense of completion that is secure in real time for our faith. Pray, study, believe and know that the war is won, and we are victorious! Is this not the completion of our faith in Jesus Christ as King of Kings and Lord of Lords? I pray that there will be a better understanding of the big picture and hopefully it will answer some questions that you may have concerning why things happen in your life. Be prepared! Your deliverance draws near!

I

THE INVINCIBLE OBEDIENT

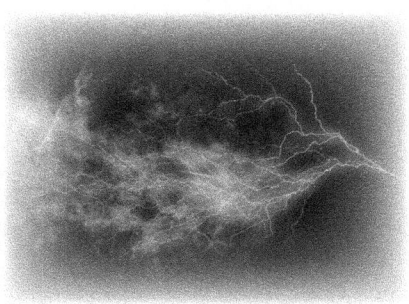

> *And He will deliver their kings into your hand, and you will destroy their name from under heaven; no one shall be able to stand against you until you have destroyed them. You shall burn the carved images of their gods with fire; you shall not covet the silver or gold that is on them, nor take it for yourselves, lest you be snared by it; for it is an abomination to the LORD your God.* **(Deuteronomy 7:24-25)**

God has given Moses specific instructions for conquering the giants in the land. In all of this, He also gives the people the incentive for success. There is no better motivational tool than to know that God is leading the armies to fight for you. Life is hard enough on your own without having your life and the lives of others be destroyed. God, in His infinite mercies and grace, send specific commands to carry out for the Israelites to be successful in conquering the land of Canaan. The commands told the people that if they would follow the Lord God and look to Him for everything, then He will hand all the armies of your enemies and the land they possessed into the hands of Israel. The Lord God fulfills everything that He has promised.

God said that *He* would deliver your enemies in your hands and *you* will destroy their name from under heaven. The last statement is very intentional and final. He said that you will destroy even their name from under heaven. This means that even the mention of their names will be erased from the record of heaven. God is not just defeating and turning them over to Israel, He is destroying the enemies and erasing them from memory. A permanent destruction, wow! This is the God that stands and fights for us. Who stands and fights with us and has our backs and strengthens us when it is needed.

The conditions set by God are not difficult to accomplish, but for a people who were immersed in the pagan cultures of the day, it becomes a great challenge to overcome. He also tells them to not only destroy the carved images but to burn them with fire. God wants the people to witness that God is the only god and there are none mightier than He. Fire is visually symbolic of purification. When He tells them to burn the idols and carved images with fire, it is part of the purification of the people. It is final when they see their idols burned to dust and ashes. The temptation of wealth was and is a true problem not only for the Israelites but for anyone who acquires wealth when it is not God ordained.

For example, in chapter seven of Joshua, it only took the sin of one person to bring defeat on the whole nation. Israel was not only defeated at Ai, but thirty-six men were truck down and the remainder of the three thousand soldiers were chased as far as Shebarim. Achan had charged into the city of Ai with the others. When he saw the royal robes, the gold and the silver, Achan coveted them and took them for himself and hid them in his tent in the ground. God told Joshua that all of Israel had sinned, but it was the sin of one man that caused their destruction. God was making a point. If you are going into the war with God, let Him call the commands and you follow them. It is simple. Achan learned a hard lesson, but he learned it with his life. The Israelites, by law, were ordered to stone him, his family, servants and anyone associated with him to death. He also ordered them to burn all his possessions to demonstrate to the people that they should be focusing and following the Lord God and no other gods. It is amazing to see the commitment in a people who experience the consequences of disobedience to the Lord God.

The message was received, as it should have been, with fear and trembling of the Lord God of Israel. The message was clear. If they follow the Lord God of Israel and follow his commands, then all the

The Battle for Eternity

things promised by Him will be fulfilled. If you choose your own path, then the consequences are death eternal. How does this help your perception of the battle for eternity? Can you be invincible? Yes! But only through obedience and faithfulness to the Lord God. He said that obedience is better than sacrifice. Sacrifice can be a one-time experience in some cases, but obedience must be your life.

GOD'S PROMISE TO DELIVER AND PROTECT

> *No man shall be able to stand before you all the days of your life; as I was with Moses, so I will be with you. I will not leave you nor forsake you. Be strong and of good courage, for to this people you shall divide as an inheritance the land which I swore to their fathers to give them.* **(Joshua 1:5-6)**

When the Christian believer attempts to battle the darkness and evil of the world alone, they stumble and fall. Mostly, they will drift away from the Lord for assorted reasons and, more precisely, excuses. The beauty of the walk with the Lord is that He is merciful and forgiving even as we are running away from Him. The greatest joy that is brought to the Lord Jesus is obedience. The whole notion of obedience brings with it the understanding that with it we can move mountains. That right! You are probably thinking, "I thought that if we had faith of a mustard seed then we could move mountains." True. Jesus said that in His teachings to the disciples. But, consider this. Apart from obedience, faith is just belief. The faith in the fact that Jesus will accomplish what He said He would do and acting on it. This is the true idea behind obedience. We trust the Lord Jesus enough to act on what He says He will do, that is faith acting in obedience. Joshua had faith in the promise of God. He said that *"No man shall be able to stand before you all the days of your life."* The Lord God has proven Himself time and again to His faithfulness to His Word. He will fulfill His promises, but in His time.

God had never given Joshua reason to doubt Him. He had been at Moses' side the whole of his time with God and experienced

God in person. Moses walked with God, but he was flawed, as all people are before a holy God. God is telling Joshua to trust Him in faith. He is calling him to lead the people of Israel in obedience to His call and His Word and He will deliver the nations into his hands. No man will stand before him, if he acts in obedience to the call of God. The next part of verse five reinforces the previous. He says that *"I will not leave you nor forsake you."* This is the promise given to us today. Three thousand five hundred years later, after Joshua conquered Canaan by the hand of God, we have the same hand of God delivering us in the battles we face with the giants in our lives. We can be invincible in our obedience to the Lord Jesus Christ and He will never leave us or forsake us. He will also lead us through our battle against the giants we face in life to victory. This should be words of comfort and strength for us all. We are not in the battle alone. The Creator of all things and the incarnate Word and Son of God is our power and strength. So, go into the battle with boldness, faith and confidence.

> ***Only be strong and very courageous, that you may observe to do according to all the law which Moses My servant commanded you; do not turn from it to the right hand or to the left, that you may prosper wherever you go. This Book of the Law shall not depart from your mouth, but you shall meditate in it day and night, that you may observe to do according to all that is written in it. For then you will make your way prosperous, and then you will have good success.* (Joshua 1:7-8)**

The life of the believer is a life of many battles. But, to win the war, you must fight one battle at a time with obedience and faith in the Lord Jesus and His commands. As the Apostle Paul says, we must stay the course and finish the race to reach the promised glory. The Lord God is telling Joshua and the people of Israel to have faith and trust in Him and observe His law and everything will be given to them as promised. This is a simple condition, but it is difficult for even those who witnessed God first hand. We look at the whole picture in the recliner at our homes in our comfortable translations of the scripture and raise the question, "how can they be so dull? How can they not be faithful and obedient to God? He was there! They heard Him and saw what they could see. The statement in verse eight set in place the fulfillment of God's promise to the people. He said that He would make their way prosperous. Even though they would not be allowed to take anything from some of the cities, in the end they would prosper. They would prosper as a nation in lands, as a people and spiritually. Following God's law and acting in obedience to His commands, you will have good success.

Joshua knew that the Lord God would make good on His word to His people. So, Joshua had no problem with faith and obedience. It was the people. Imagine how difficult it would be to have over a million people agree on and stand behind one thing. In churches today, it is next to impossible to have two or more agree on anything, even though we are commanded to do it. Joshua was successful when he conquered Canaan, except for the incident at Ai with Achan. But, even that act of disobedience was a lesson learned for the people of Israel. They knew from that point forward that obedience made for a much greater success than disobedience. Every city that Joshua and the Israelites conquered, if they followed God's plan they were successful. If they altered it in any way, their destruction was imminent. Is it possible to be an invincible obedient follower of Jesus Christ? Absolutely! Is it easy to do? By no means! But, we are given the encouraging words found in the Book of Joshua to give us strength. We also stand strong because we an advocate with the Father, Jesus Christ our Lord and Savior.

> *Have I not commanded you? Be strong and of good courage; do not be afraid, nor be dismayed, for the LORD your God is with you wherever you go.* **(Joshua 1:9)**

The Lord has commanded us to be strong and very courageous in the spiritual battles that confront us in our everyday lives. If we do not believe that spiritual warfare real, just look at the news and on the internet. Look in our own communities and the rise in crime. The end is near and we as Christians must take every moment of our day seriously spiritually. Meditate even more in the Word of God, pray and seek the face of the Lord Jesus while He can be found. The amazing thing about God is that He is with us wherever we go. The end of verse nine is confirmation of this and should build our faith to serve our Lord in spirit and truth.

Found in approaching God in prayer

> ***For this reason I bow my knees to the Father of our Lord Jesus Christ, from whom the whole family in heaven and earth is named, that He would grant you, according to the riches of His glory, to be strengthened with might through His Spirit in the inner man, that Christ may dwell in your hearts through faith; that you, being rooted and grounded in love, may be able to comprehend with all the saints what is the width and length and depth and height—* (Ephesians 3:14-18)**

The greatest defense we have in the war for our souls is prayer. Not just any flippant prayer but true spiritual prayer from the heart. If you know Paul's history, you will note that he is a powerful man of God and that prayer is the cornerstone of his strength. Prayer is the strength in the relationship that we develop with the Lord Jesus Christ. Notice the way he prays for the Ephesian church. He looks to the glory and majesty of the Lord God for strength. The Ephesian church during Paul's time was strong and growing. Paul was very faithful in his obedience to the Lord and in many accounts, he was, it seemed, invincible. Despite persecution, Paul was faithful to fulfill every task the Lord Jesus Christ called him to do, regardless of the cost.

His prayer was for the people of God to be faithful and have the same confidence that he had in them and in the Lord Jesus Christ. First, he prayed that they would be strengthened with might through the Holy Spirit active in their lives. Are we actively pursuing the power of God through obedience in the Lord? Next, he prayed that Christ would dwell in their hearts. This is something that is lacking in the Christian's life today. When Christ dwells in your heart, He is continually at the forefront of your life. Everything you do, say and even think should be focused on Christ and Him alone. The only way we can do this is through true faith in Christ. All of this is so they will be rooted and grounded in love. But, not just any love. The love of God. The love that nailed Jesus, the Son of God, on that wretched cross for our sins. If we do this, then we will truly understand the whole spectrum of God's grace and mercy.

> *To know the love of Christ which passes knowledge; that you may be filled with all the fullness of God.* **(Ephesians 3:19)**

The experience of God's love is known through the love of Christ and His sacrifice which passes all knowledge. I find that interesting because I am one who has studied for years in academics concerning Biblical and theological understandings. But, even with a research Masters in Historical Theology, I am drawn to the basics of scripture and the teachings of my Lord Jesus Christ and His love to give me strength in times of trials. He said that through the love of Christ you may be filled with all the fullness of God. Wow! Amazing love, how can it be? My Savior will love a wretch like me. We do not understand even a fraction of the love God the Father has for us. But, we can be obedient. Through full obedience to God and His call, we are reflecting the love of Christ in obedience and in this we are invincible. I do not know everything or presume to have all the answers to anything Biblical or otherwise, but it is through the power and knowledge in the Holy Spirit that I am guided in everyday life and experiences. Praise the Lord for His most marvelous gift!

> *"Nevertheless I tell you the truth. It is to your advantage that I go away; for if I do not go away, the Helper will not come to you; but if I depart, I will send Him to you. And when He has come, He will convict the world of sin, and of righteousness, and of judgment: of sin, because they do not*

> *believe in Me; of righteousness, because I go to My Father and you see Me no more; of judgment, because the ruler of this world is judged."* **(John 16:7-11)**

The desire to be invincible is a natural human desire from childhood. But, realistically, there is no practical worldly realization of that dream for your life. We believe that invincibility is for comic heroes like superman and wonder woman. In the spiritual world, invincibility is found in obedience to the call and the Will of God. Faith is the cornerstone of a life rooted in obedience to the Father. So, the Holy Spirit is sent to lead the battles in the spiritual realm so the you can lead a stronger, godly life. The description in this passage is truly speaking to the strength of the Holy Spirit in the life of the believer. He is describing the role of the Holy Spirit and the way that we need to understand the power the Spirit of God has in the world. The ruler of this world is defeated. Believing that the ruler of this world is defeated, gives power and strength to the battle for eternity.

The disciples, while Jesus was saying these things, were very confused about what Jesus was saying to them. They believed that Jesus was the Son of God and therefore He was invincible and would never leave them. Keep in mind, Jesus walked with them over those three years teaching and demonstrating His Godly power and authority. In their hearts, they knew Him as God and there was no way they could have access to that sort of power. But, Jesus was telling them that His relationship with them had grown and that He was going to give them the same power and authority He possesses.

THE PRAYER OF THE OBEDIENT

> *And when you pray, you shall not be like the hypocrites. For they love to pray standing in the synagogues and on the corners of the streets, that they may be seen by men. Assuredly, I say to you, they have their reward. But you, when you pray, go into your room, and when you have shut your*

> *door, pray to your Father who is in the secret place; and your Father who sees in secret will reward you openly. And when you pray, do not use vain repetitions as the heathen do. For they think that they will be heard for their many words.*
> **(Matthew 6:5-7)**

In everything we do as Christians, there are ways of loving the Lord God, but the most effective and affinitive ways of service is through obedience. People in the world criticize those who refer to themselves as Christians and say that our obedience to God is a blind faith. We know that we have a God who truly loves us and empowers us for His glory. Our obedience is based on a faith through evidence found in our lives and in scripture. Prayer is our response to the faithful obedience we have before the Father, the Son and through the Holy Spirit. Jesus is teaching us to be humble when we pray. The more humble, the more powerful! This is the way to be invincible in a world that is determined to see your destruction. The paradoxes of the Christian life set us at odds with the world and its teachings. Humility gives rise to power and pride brings destruction.

When Jesus taught this portion of His teaching to His disciples on prayer, He was beginning His ministry and establishing the foundation for a Godly way of life. Prayer is the cornerstone of an invincibly obedient life in Christ. In the battle for eternity, it is bloody battle that is fought best in the hands of the Lord Jesus Christ and in the power and authority of the Holy Spirit. The greatest weapons at the Christian's disposal are faithful and obedient prayer, fasting, and fervent study of the scriptures. The key to a successful prayer life is found in faithful obedience. Jesus said not to be prideful and wordy in your prayers. It is the condition of your heart and not what you say. Many times, Jesus reprimanded the religious leaders of His day concerning the way they called attention to themselves in everything to demonstrate their piety. This is not what God wants to hear from His people. When attempting to understand the best way to pray, reflect on the beatitudes. The beatitudes are not just a guide and a goal, but they are truth in life.

People in churches today who consider themselves righteous need to take a close look at the Jesus' reference in a parable of Luke chapter eighteen verse nine, ***"Also He spoke this parable to some who trusted in themselves that they were righteous, and despised others:"*** He began this parable of the Pharisee and the Tax Collector directing it to a specific type of people. We call these the "self-righteous" people. These are those who find themselves more pious or spiritual than anyone else in the congregation. Does this sound familiar? Are there those in your congregation who are like these people? There are two people here who Jesus is characterizing. The first is the Pharisee. The Pharisee is the ruler of the Temple and he has full authority in the synagogue as well. He effectively enforces the rules and regulations regarding the Jewish people in accordance to the Book of the Law. They are legalistic and narrow-mind in their approach to understanding of the law. Therefore, they totally missed Jesus when He walked and taught in their midst. They were the pious of the leaders of the Jewish people. So, Jesus, when he began the parable, He spoke to the specific audience of which He was speaking, interesting.

> *"Two men went up to the temple to pray, one a Pharisee and the other a tax collector. The Pharisee stood and prayed thus with himself, 'God, I thank You that I am not like other men—extortioners, unjust, adulterers, or even as this tax collector. I fast twice a week; I give tithes of all that I possess.'"* **(Luke 18:10-12)**

The Pharisee was a self-righteous ruler of the Temple. He believed since he was a Pharisee that he should command respect. He was also considered more righteous and pious than anyone else because of his status and rank. He believed that God saw it this way as well. Notice how Jesus described his stature before the Lord God. His attitude was focused inward and not upward. He said that the Pharisee stood and prayed. He did not take a posture of humility and reverence before God. Then, he prayed with himself. When those who arise within the congregation overwhelming those who are praying, is it the Spirit of God moving or the spirit of the self-righteous Pharisee in us all. They may not realize that it is being disruptive. Jesus also said that we should not do things to cause our brother or sister to stumble. Many times, if there are those who complain about the ones who are loudly praying in the spirit, then they are considered less spiritual. On the other side of the coin, those who are locked in their outmoded ways, they are truly legalistic in every way in concern for the church. The Pharisees fall into both these examples. They are the coin and a classic example of the hard and loveless Christian.

> *"And the tax collector, standing afar off, would not so much as raise his eyes to heaven, but beat his breast, saying, 'God, be merciful to me a sinner!'"* **(Luke 18:13)**

The next character in this parable was the tax collector. The tax collector was among the most despised of those people in that time. They were ruthless and were out for nobody but themselves. Their lives revolved around monetary gain. But, Matthew, one of Jesus' most trusted among His disciples, was a tax collector. Also, one of the more unforgiving tax collectors of the time, Zacchaeus, who was the chief tax collector and was rich (Luke 19:1-10). Jesus stirred the pot with the Pharisees when He went and spent time with Zacchaeus in his home. Obedience, Jesus set the example how to obey when it came to the Lord and His call. The difference between the two men was their attitudes and understanding concerning sin. The Pharisee was engrossed in his own righteousness and piousness, so he did not understand nor believe that he was a sinner. The tax collector, on the other hand, humbly knew of his true state of sinfulness and was repentant.

> *"I tell you, this man went down to his house justified rather than the other; for everyone who exalts himself will be humbled, and he who humbles himself will be exalted."* **(Luke 18:14)**

This was a pointed statement from Jesus to those who considered themselves holier than others. It was also a message to those who humbly believe they will never achieve the love of God and that they are unworthy of mercy. In the words, in this verse, Jesus speaks to both these ideological groups of Christians. You are saying, "Christians?" Yes, Christians. If you think hard and scan your congregation, you will probably find a cross-section of the culture that you see outside the church. Why? Because we are all sinners saved by grace and it is only through the grace and mercy of Jesus Christ that we are worthy to walk through the doors of a sanctified house of God. So, examine yourselves carefully. We need to take Luke eighteen verse fourteen seriously as we consider our Christian walk with the Lord Jesus Christ. I, as a pastor, do not consider myself more righteous or important than any other member of the congregation that Jesus has entrusted me with, even though my responsibility to God and His people is held to a higher standard. We as pastors must understand that we are held to a higher standard and that we are the examples to those who need a standard to witness for strength and encouragement. Looking at the prayers of the obedient, there must be seen the component of true humility. The power of the prayer of the obedient rests in their faith that they will stand firm in the Lord Jesus Christ and that in Christ we can be invincible before our enemies.

BLESSINGS PROMISED THE OBEDIENT

> *And Moses went up to God, and the LORD called to him from the mountain, saying, "Thus you shall say to the house of Jacob, and tell the children of Israel: 'You have seen what I did to the Egyptians, and how I bore you on eagles' wings and brought you to Myself. Now therefore, if you will indeed obey My voice and keep My covenant, then you shall be a special treasure to Me above all people; for all the earth is Mine. And you shall be to Me a kingdom of priests and a holy nation.' These are the words which you shall speak to the children of Israel."* **(Exodus 19:3-6)**

God delivered the people of Israel out of bondage. He called them from the darkness of this world into the light of His redemption. Is this not what He wants to accomplish in us? In the story of the exodus of God's people, God heard them, delivered them from bondage and set their feet on a solid foundation with Him. He told them the plans He made and the reason for the chosen. Why would you think the people were so reluctant to follow God even after all they have witnessed? It is easy for you and me to make such blanketed judgements on people who like over four millennia ago, but the truth is that we are no different. In fact, we are probably worse because we have the written records easily accessible to us and we still have a tough time believing He will keep His promises. God made a basic three-part statement to Moses and the people of Israel. First, He told them to remember what He did for them. Second, He asked them to obey His voice. This implies that God will continue to build the relationship that He desires between He and His people, a personal relationship. Finally, He said for them to keep His Covenant with them.

The Covenant is a contract or binding agreement between two or more people to achieve a common outcome or result. The common outcome or result that was set to be accomplished was deliverance and redemption. God saw that the deliverance was the actual beginning of the covenant and the redemption was the result. Redemption, as God viewed it, was in terms of reconciliation back to the perfect and right relationship He had in the beginning of creation before the fall. The Covenant usually has both an "if" and a "then" that establishes the perimeters of the contract. When God makes a covenant, He will not break that agreement. We, on the other hand, are prone to looking for loopholes and finding ways of breaking contracts. God has our best interests at heart and only wants what is best for us. Humanity is engrained within the sinful nature the propensity for selfish desires, even when they are wrong. But, God said that if the people did those three things, then He would make them a special treasure above all other nations of the earth. Also, He said that they would be a kingdom of priests and a holy nation. Because of this, God is saying that they would be blessed. Today, we read our scriptures and say, why is this so wrong, how did they not want this or even see what God is doing? It is easy to see God's plan and even the big picture when you can open the scripture anytime you want, but they did not have this convenience. Their perspective was much different.

> ***"Hear, O Israel: The LORD our God, the LORD is one! You shall love the LORD your God with all your heart, with all your soul, and with all your strength. And these words which I command you today shall be in your heart."*** **(Deuteronomy 6:4-6)**

The concept of obedience to a holy God is a notion of oneness of heart with God. There is no way you can fail if you are one with the Lord our God. Jesus never second-guessed the Father on anything, even death on the cross. God is saying here that we must love Him with all our being. We cannot be fragmented in our loyalties to Him. If we are fragmented in our loyalties to Him, then we cannot be living in full obedience to Him. In everything we are and do in our lives, we must be covenanted with Him in obedience. Let us strive to be like Him in all respects and that we will not fail to love and obey Him in all things. When we do this, we can consider to be invincible in mind and soul and perfect in the eyes of a Holy God in Christ Jesus. Are you ready and willing to do this in your life?

2

THE CONFLICT

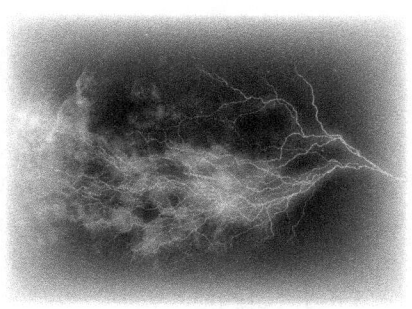

> *For I delight in the law of God according to the inward man. But I see another law in my members, warring against the law of my mind, and bringing me into captivity to the law of sin which is in my members. O wretched man that I am! Who will deliver me from this body of death? I thank God—through Jesus Christ our Lord!*
> *So then, with the mind I myself serve the law of God, but with the flesh the law of sin.* **(Romans 7:22-25)**

The conflict within the believer is the struggle that everyone faces daily, but it is the way they approach the battle that sets them apart. The common Christian does not understand that there is a battle they are at the center of and they are oblivious to the fact that it is even occurring. The people of God are so distracted by the material issues that slam them daily, they are unaware of the horrific war that is raging around them for their souls. Many preachers and teachers who are called according to the grace of God are delivering a message that is "watered down" and inoffensive. Why?! There are feel good messages given to large congregations all over the world. Christians today, in denominational circles, are extremely tolerant of the things of the world for the sake of inclusiveness.

Paul's message in the passage in Romans seven is very open and truthful to his own condition. The gospel message is offensive to those with sin in their lives. If you say that you do not sin, then you are a liar and Jesus Christ is not Lord and Savior of your life. The Apostle Paul is giving the reader of the letter a picture of the humble heart that is focused toward God in all things. Are you "all in" with your Christian faith and focused on Him and Him alone? Are you focused on yourself and the gospel message does not affect you in any way? He was giving us a glimpse at the true struggle that everyone faces every day. The struggle of loving and serving the world and not the Lord is a common one. But, as Paul tells us, it is the law of God that we are made aware of that gives us the option to take the different path. Those who follow the law of sin and death are not aware, most of the time, that they are travelling a road straight to eternal damnation. Even though we all travel this road every day, Paul tells the believer that we have a choice.

> *There is therefore now no condemnation to those who are in Christ Jesus, who do not walk according to the flesh, but according to the Spirit. For the law of the Spirit of life in Christ Jesus has made me free from the law of sin and death.* **(Romans 8:1-2)**

The Apostle Paul drew on his connection and intimate relationship with the Lord Jesus Christ in all his life and ministry. We, as Christians, should follow the example of one who walked on both sides of the fence and lived whole-heartedly his life in both camps. Despite all that Paul was in his life, he was as much committed to the spreading of the gospel of Christ to the world. Paul witnessed the stoning of the disciple Stephen and the radiance that shone from his face even amid his mortality and painful persecution (Acts 6:15). The picture of that moment was, I believe, etched in his mind for the remainder of his days. Therefore, we can look at this as a revelation of Paul to the believer. He not only believed everything that preached, but he lived it as well. The life of the Apostle Paul reflected the life that Christ had intended the Christian to live.

The belief that there is no condemnation to those who are in Christ Jesus is the cornerstone of our foundation. Why? Because, if we are truly *in* Christ Jesus, then we are focused on Him and Him alone. The beauty of this statement is found in the simplicity of the message. If we are in Christ Jesus, then nothing else matters in our lives. For example, when you dated, you focused every waking moment on how you can make that special someone happy. Our relationship with Jesus Christ should be even more because we are striving for eternal life with Jesus. The problem is with the attitude in which we approach the relationship. Jesus enters the relationship unconditionally, whereas, we enter conditionally. The conflict is found in the attitude and condition of our heart. We enter the relationship with a desired outcome and the timeline set by us. The wonderful aspect of Jesus' love for us is that we will continuously fall away for the same reason, yet Jesus, time and time again receives us back. If we are wronged in a relationship, then we will get out of the relationship and seek another that will form to our ways and beliefs. Aren't you glad Jesus does not give up on us? Amen!

Paul goes on to define what he means by being "in" Christ Jesus. First, he says that this person is one who does not walk after the flesh. Remember, the struggle of chapter seven that Paul fought was a battle between flesh and spirit. All conflict that we experience is found in the spiritual realm. The battle rages relentlessly within us daily. Satan finds the easiest means by which to defeat us, Christian or not, is to introduce fear and doubt to our faith. The Bible defines faith as *"the substance of things hoped for, the evidence of things not seen."* **(Hebrews 11:1)** The whole basis of our faith is found in the promise of eternal life and the present life lived in Christ Jesus. The Hebrew believers that the writer of Hebrews was writing to were those who sought after the eternal faith found in Christ Jesus amid persecution. So, for the believer to believe in eternal life and abundant present life, there needs to be a firm belief that have victory in the spiritual battle that we are engaged.

> *I beseech you therefore, brethren, by the mercies of God, that you present your bodies a living sacrifice, holy, acceptable to God, which is your reasonable service. And do not be conformed to this world, but be transformed by the renewing of your mind, that you may prove what is that good and acceptable and perfect will of God.* **(Romans 12:1-2)**

This passage in Romans chapter twelve sets the stage for the climax of the Christ-like life. If you then live this life, then you will be willing to present yourselves as living sacrifices before a living God and a lost and dying world. Being a living sacrifice for God is a daily endeavor. The sacrifices of old only temporarily sufficed and atoned for the sinful nature of the spiritual life of the individual. Then, when a sacrifice was presented, it could not be repeated with the same offering. But, now, we can offer ourselves daily as living sacrifices. Living in accordance with the commands and statutes of God and not a one-time plan. God made His one-time sacrifice for all time in His Son Jesus on the cross. The ultimate sacrifice for all sins of the entire world was made by God in His Son as an example for us all. We could never truly repay the eternal sacrifice God made through His Son for us. All God the Father wants from us is for us to Love and obey His Son. There is no greater love than this that a man would lay down his life for his friends. Should we be living sacrifices for our Lord and Savior Jesus Christ? He did it for you! Yes!

When we present ourselves as living sacrifices before God, we must be holy and acceptable to God. Therefore, the manner that we serve says more about us and our relationship with Christ than anything else. If we are to be living sacrifices, then that means that we will sacrifice our lives both physically and spiritually daily. We are not in the fight alone. It is a conflict that has been raging from the very beginning. The question that it raised in our minds is "what difference would I make?" Or, we would ask a question like, "Why should I even fight a fight that I cannot possibly win?" The answer is simple. You are not fighting alone because God the Father, God the Son, and God the Holy Spirit are fighting for you and with you. This is the war for your soul and you should take a stake in the battle and especially the outcome!

> **Finally, my brethren, be strong in the Lord and in the power of His might. Put on the whole armor of God, that you may be able to stand against the wiles of the devil. For we do not wrestle against flesh and blood, but against princi-**

> *palities, against powers, against the rulers of the darkness of this age, against spiritual hosts of wickedness in the heavenly places.* **(Ephesians 6:10-12)**

Recognizing the warriors in the fight is what makes your defenses strong. The offense that we have as our strength is far greater than any that will ever come against in the battle for eternity. God is our Lord God and Jesus, His Son, our commander and chief. When the angels and archangels came to the defense of Israel, God's chosen people, the physical enemies of Israel were unaware of the innumerable army that stood at the ready before them. The conflict that we are engaged in is for all time. The Christian today has no idea of the extent and to the length the battles are reaching to save each individual soul. Both sides of the war are having great loses and have received great losses since the beginning of time. Yes, the war is about saving humanity, God's most precious creation, from total annihilation by the evil forces of the adversary. The way God the Father sees it is that each individual soul is as important as the next. Good, bad indifferent to Him, He loves them all and does not want any of them to be destroyed in their sin but to live an abundant life eternally with Him. This is the whole reason that Jesus, God's Son, had to come, live and die because redemption can only come through the Son and His ultimate sacrifice.

BATTLING YOUR GIANTS: DAVID AND GOLIATH

> *Then David said to the Philistine, "You come to me with a sword, with a spear, and with a javelin. But I come to you in the name of the LORD of hosts, the God of the armies of Israel, whom you have defied. This day the LORD will deliver you into my hand, and I will strike you and take your head from you. And this day I will give the carcasses of the camp of the Philistines to the birds of the air and the wild beasts of the earth, that all the earth may know that there is a God in Israel. Then all this assembly shall know that the LORD does not save with sword and spear; for the battle is*

the Lord's, and He will give you into our hands." **(1 Samuel 17:45-47)**

David was a teenager at best, he knew from where the power came to defeat the enemy despite the size and enormous strength of the foe. We as Christians must stand and fight in the faith regardless the cost. There must be a realization that the battle is not ours but the Lord's. He said that we would endure persecution, but the Lord Jesus is mightier than anything the adversary will attack with in your life. David knew this going into the conflict with Goliath and stood strong in faith that God would be victorious. Are you stepping battle knowing that God is the one who will make you victorious? Goliath was a true giant, with gear, standing about nine feet tall at best figures. David was, at best, half his height. God brings victory against the most insurmountable odds. This declares God's glory. David told Goliath, "This day the Lord will deliver you into my hand, and I will strike you and take your head from you." The prediction was a statement of faith and David truly believed what he was saying. God was true to David's word. He is also true to our word and our actions as we act in faith toward giants.

> *It is God who arms me with strength,*
> *And makes my way perfect.*
> *He makes my feet like the feet of deer,*
> *And sets me on my high places.*
> *He teaches my hands to make war,*
> *So that my arms can bend a bow of bronze.*
> *You have also given me the shield of Your salvation;*
> *Your right hand has held me up,*
> *Your gentleness has made me great.*
> **(Psalm 18:32-35)**

David reflects in the eighteenth Psalm about those who would come against him. More important, he reflects on the fact that God is the one who prepares for the battles of your life. He is giving glory to the Lord God for His faithfulness to him and the way He prepares us for the conflict even before it takes place. Despite our moments of weakness, God holds us steady in His hands and delivers us when we are faithful to Him.

> ***And he shall say to them, 'Hear, O Israel: Today you are on the verge of battle with your enemies. Do not let your heart faint, do not be afraid, and do not tremble or be terrified because of them; for the LORD your God is He who goes with you, to fight for you against your enemies, to save you.'*** **(Deuteronomy 20:3-4)**

We are engaged in battles every moment of every day. Yet, the Lord God tells us to not let your heart grow faint. When we are at our weakest, this is the point that He is strongest in our lives. Our nature is to hold on to every aspect of our lives until our dying breath. Is this the eternal realistic goals and aims? No! God wants us to serve Him and trust Him with everything in our lives. Yes, the battle is raging, even as we speak and are weak in our flesh. He also tells us not to be afraid and do not tremble or be terrified because of our enemies. Why? Because the Lord your God is the only one that will go with you, fight for you, and save you from your enemies.

We may not be able to see the battles raging in an eternal war, but it is real. If you do not believe that the battles exist, then you are not familiar with the scripture and the many times that God intervened on behalf of His people. We are His people and He is defending us as well. We must believe and know that the heavenly hosts and the armies of the Most High God are in a real war for you. Many churches and denominations today do not believe or just dismiss the notion of the demonic or the angelic beings because it is far beyond their scope of understanding. It is believed as good stories on a page in the Bible for encouragement and empowerment. But, whether you believe monsters or Santa Clause or any other "mythical" creature is real. Start by recognizing that at the core of any of these stories is a thread, so be it so fine a thread, of truth as a basis for the story. But even more powerful than these are the ones who came from God Almighty and that exercise His

Will and answer to His authority and will defeat those battling for your soul, Amen!

ELISHA CALLS TO THE LORD GOD

> *Therefore he sent horses and chariots and a great army there, and they came by night and surrounded the city. And when the servant of the man of God arose early and went out, there was an army, surrounding the city with horses and chariots. And his servant said to him, "Alas, my master! What shall we do?"* **(2 Kings 6:14-15)**

The simplicity of this event in the ministry of the prophet Elisha was truly one of great power. The servant of Elisha was stressed because the Syrian armies had encamped around the city and they were surrounded. Fear had begun to take its toll on him. But Elisha knew that God had the battle won before it had begun. The vast Syrian army at the time was noted for their ruthlessness in battle and would surely destroy the city and kill everyone in the city. The question asked by the servant of Elisha was a legitimate one. Elisha, full of faith and the Spirit of God, prayed to the Lord God of Israel to open his servant's eyes so he may see the glory of the heavenly hosts that surrounded them. We are not alone, and we do not fight alone in this fight. The Lord God said to Joshua before the conquest of Canaan, "Be strong and very courageous, for I will never leave you or forsake you." This is His statement to us every day!

> *So he answered, "Do not fear, for those who are with us are more than those who are with them." And Elisha prayed, and said, "LORD, I pray, open his eyes that he may see." Then the LORD opened the eyes of the young man, and he saw. And behold, the mountain was full of horses and chariots of fire all around Elisha. So when the Syrians came down to him, Elisha prayed to the LORD, and said, "Strike this people, I pray, with blindness." And He struck them with blindness according to the word of Elisha.* **(2 Kings 6:14-18)**

The enemy of our Lord will never accept defeat until Christ comes and throws him into the bottomless pit and the lake of fire for eternal torment. When the servant looked around, he saw the mountains ablaze with horses and chariots of fire as the glory of the Lord God was ready for battle and the defense of His people. Remember that Elisha did not pray to the Lord God to smite the Syrians, but he prayed that they would be stricken with blindness. He did not want the soldiers to die but to be taught a lesson in the power of God. In the cases where there was intervention on behalf of enemies, it is a lesson in mercy and grace that we need to heed to in the Christian life today. Elisha saw the redemption and the mighty hand of God and he prayed for the Lord to stay His vengeance and show mercy. The Lord's hand of mercy is mightier than that of the sword. This also shows the compassion of Elisha toward the people who would have otherwise easy defeated them. We as Christians need to learn from this for the understanding that God wants to give grace and mercy, but He is just as mighty with the sword.

The most amazing example of God's vengeance was during the reign of Hezekiah when the forces of Sennacherib, King of Assyria, had surrounded the city of Jerusalem:

> *For I will defend this city, to save it For My own sake and for My servant David's sake.'"*
> *And it came to pass on a certain night that the angel of the LORD went out, and killed in the camp of the Assyrians one hundred and eighty-five thousand; and when people arose early in the morning, there were the corpses—all dead.* **(2 Kings 19:34-35)**

The Assyrian armies were the most formidable of the time. They were feared by all the nations of the known world. The Lord God had known the heart of Hezekiah as he prayed. Hezekiah had a heart focused on God even in times of inevitable defeat. As we know, there is no God greater than our God and His power is more than we can fathom. He sent an Angel of the Lord into the camp and in a single night, the angel killed one-hundred eighty-five thousands of Sennacherib's strongest forces. One angel of the Lord, in a single night, destroyed an entire army. The largest and most powerful in the known world. Imagine, what do you think the Lord is capable of with the entire heavenly hosts? We have the heavenly hosts at our call if we are in need and our hearts are focused and true to Him in obedience.

The Lord God told Hezekiah of the impending fate of Sennacherib and his massive elite forces. He told them, through the prophet Isaiah, Isaiah 37, that not only would Sennacherib be defeated, but he would die in his own land. God sees our distress and answers the prayers of the faithful warrior of God. If you are faithful to Him in the insignificant things, then He will give you mighty things.

With God All Things Are Possible

> *Then Jesus said to His disciples, "Assuredly, I say to you that it is hard for a rich man to enter the kingdom of heaven. And again I say to you, it is easier for a camel to go through the eye of a needle than for a rich man to enter the kingdom of God."*
>
> *When His disciples heard it, they were greatly astonished, saying, "Who then can be saved?"*
>
> *But Jesus looked at them and said to them, "With men this is impossible, but with God all things are possible."*
>
> *Then Peter answered and said to Him, "See, we have left all and followed You. Therefore what shall we have?"*
>
> *So Jesus said to them, "Assuredly I say to you, that in the regeneration, when the Son of Man sits on the throne of His glory, you who have followed Me will also sit on twelve thrones, judging the twelve tribes of Israel. And everyone who has left houses or brothers or sisters or father or mother or wife or children or lands, for My name's sake, shall receive a hundredfold, and inherit eternal life. But many who are first will be last, and the last first."* **(Matthew 19:23-30)**

The Battle for Eternity

The way in which we can defeat our enemies is to realize that we need to put Him first and give everything to Him. We are like the disciples in our misunderstandings of God's love for us and all that He is prepared to do for us. He has defeated sin and death when Jesus died on the cross and was resurrected for our sins. This is the redemption and how the enemies of our Lord God are defeated. The conflict we are in the middle of is real. If you are a child of God through the shed blood of His Son Jesus Christ, then your enemies are the enemies of the Lord Jesus Christ and the heavenly hosts are ready to fight for the single soul to enter heaven. Jesus told the disciples that in the regeneration, when the Son of Man sits on the throne of His glory, all who follow Him will sit there as well and rule because of their faithfulness even to the death. The point of what Jesus was telling them was that the disciples were struggling with why Jesus would even question their faithfulness to Him. He was teaching them a hard lesson in humility. Jesus tells us to deny ourselves and follow Him. This is contrary to the teachings of the world. The example is to follow the interaction with the rich young ruler and his reluctance to give up everything to the poor and follow Jesus. We are the rich young man in our Christian lives. There is a reluctance to give everything to Jesus, to give it all up for the sake of the gospel of Jesus Christ. Do you truly believe? Are you going through the motions? Do you think that your "fire insurance" is paid so you do not have to worry about anything? You better think again! The battle is raging, and it is ***your*** choice to follow Him. Do not assume that your battle is won! If you turn away from Him, then He can turn away from you. Remember, the Lord God lifted His presence from the Temple and the people of God for Nebuchadnezzar, King of Babylon, to conquer Jerusalem and destroy the Temple. So, we should not presume to think that God will not remove His presence. He will remove it because of our unfaithfulness and His justice.

> ***Then I heard a loud voice saying in heaven, "Now salvation, and strength, and the kingdom of our God, and the power of His Christ have come, for the accuser of our breth-***

ren, who accused them before our God day and night, has been cast down. And they overcame him by the blood of the Lamb and by the word of their testimony, and they did not love their lives to the death. Therefore rejoice, O heavens, and you who dwell in them! Woe to the inhabitants of the earth and the sea! For the devil has come down to you, having great wrath, because he knows that he has a short time."
(Revelation 12:10-12)

The power of God is found in the Christ. The devil and his forces are no match for the heavenly hosts. Do not sell the power short because the devil, the Satan, Lucifer, is defenseless against the power of almighty God and His Christ. Those who overcome the evil one, the adversary, by the blood of the Lamb and by the word of their testimony will have victory because they did not love their lives even to death. They stood strong in the battles and every conflict for the sake of the gospel of Jesus Christ, regardless of the cost. The Apostle John saw the time that we live in now. Do you think you can stand strong for the gospel of Christ and in the power of His might? As the battles intensify, the enemy's hatred for the people of God is growing more wrathful because he knows that his time is short. He wants to take as many down with him as he can. Therefore we, as Christians, must stand strong in the testimony of the gospel of Jesus Christ. We are cleansed white by the blood of the Lamb who was slain but lives and sits on His throne in the heavens. The war is not a war of flesh and blood but against the powers of darkness in the spiritual realm. Remember that what you bind on earth it is bound in the heavens. As the battles rage in our mind and hearts, it is a never-ending war for your soul and the souls of all humanity. Satan as he rages in wrath against the children of God, he knows that the war has been won through Jesus Christ and His blood. Considering this idea, he has nothing to lose and is never ceasing at his attacks to drag as many souls to hell with him as possible.

THE CHURCH IN CONFLICT EVEN TODAY

I have worked in churches with and looked up to several pastors who were preaching one way and living another. It is disheartening to see the damage spiritually to a church congregation when a pastor or leader they looked up to falls promptly into sin. A pastor, that I worked for in central Florida, was secretly having liaisons with various women in the community. He was controlling leader and presence at the church. He drove to Kentucky and interviewed me personally for the position of Education Director in a church with over one thousand members. This was my first job outside of Seminary and it was intense for me and my wife. We are taught in the scriptures to resist the devil and he will flee from you. None of us on staff ever knew the whole story, but once he was asked to resign, everyone that he brought on staff was fair game. The new pastor had an innovative approach to ministry, which I was willing to be an active participant. But, the obvious reason for this pastor was to downsize the staff.

I literally would sit in Administrative board meetings while the board members would say things like, "why are they even here? Why should they stay in church housing?" My first reaction to this is to jump up and say to them, "look, you brought us here! You interviewed us and the church now is growing!" But I kept my mouth shut and took the abuse and ridicule from something that I knew nothing about. The new pastor and the chairman of the pastor-parish relations committee called me to the office one night about eight o'clock. It was a short meeting that was a termination meeting. They said that the evangelism events were costing the church too much money and that they have decided to let me go. They said that should be able to find a church that needed an evangelism director because they saw that was my heart and passion. The problem was that they did not want it there at that church.

This was not an isolated incident in my ministry. Because I was let go from a church, no other church in the country would touch me. We even drove to St. Louis, Missouri for an interview.

I knew when I got there that this was not the place God wanted us. The people were great and very accommodating, but we knew that was not the place for us. It was like at every turn the adversary was trying to defeat us. Because I was terminated for doing my job brought up more questions than answers, which was the deal breaker. Meanwhile back in central Florida, in the same town where I worked, an outreach ministry took me in. Because I had been heavily involved with various Civic organizations and was the organizer of outreach and evangelism, they saw me as a good fit for the organization. As things progressed, the organization grew and became more self-sufficient and with the growth came more disorganization and malcontent. Through this organization I was introduced to a wonderful woman pastor who was truly and woman of God.

I became a licensed minister in the Pentecostal Holiness denomination. I taught adult Sunday School and on occasion could preach. I enjoyed teaching more than preaching, but I was learning more about ministry from a unique perspective. To make a long story short, Sunday morning as I arrived at the church and was walking up to the church, and the pastor's son walked up to me in the parking lot and told me that they had no need for me anymore. He felt that it was best for me just to leave and not return. After serving two years there, following my release from the other church, my spiritual ego took a hit. The good part with this church was that it was voluntary and not paid. After this, I could some time off from church to do some soul searching. It had seemed that the adversary had won this battle. He was not going to win the war!

After eight years in central Florida, I felt that it was time to make a change in my life. My mom had just passed away. The family and I come back home to Alabama for the funeral. I was given an opportunity for a job in maintenance at a local hospital. Moving back, we struggled for a while. So, we began to go to church where I grew up until I was married and moved away. Much of the experiences of central Florida and even some from Kentucky prepared me for much of what I was about to experience in this church. The people in the church were those that had known all my life from childhood. There lies a different dynamic all together. Even though it was about a thirty-minute drive one way, it was a fresh new experience, until the new pastor came after we had been there for two years. The pastor came in with an attitude of controlling everybody and everything. The first order of business was to fire the church secretary. This woman's family was among the charter members and founders of this church in the early part of the twentieth century. It did not settle well with the rest of the congregation. We knew what was next on the list, and because we were living Mobile, we sought a church more local for us.

A man that I worked at the hospital with then invited me and my family to his church. So, we went to visit his church. It was dynamic with a charismatic preacher and worship was powerful. We decided start going because it was half the distance and the services were empowering. After about a year of going consistently, we became members. Then about three years later, I became a deacon in the church as well an adult Sunday School teacher. Now the Lord God had finally led us to a truly Godly church to serve. We were both excited, because of all that we had experienced from previous churches this church was a breath of fresh air. But, the world and the prince of this world would soon find his way in. As I was serving as deacon, the pastor, whom I respected highly, decided that he did not love his wife anymore and divorced her. Both were highly motivated and driven in the church. The deacons met with him and tried to encourage him to seek family counseling. It seemed that we were hearing blame from both sides. As this was transpiring, the church was fracturing and dividing under the weight of the news of the break up. He stayed long enough for the rumors and accusations to reach a boiling point. He announced during his sermon on Mother's Day that he was going to take a sabbatical. Then the following fall he tendered his letter of resignation.

After searching the association that the church was a member, they looked within for a new pastor. I had been interim pastor for the previous six months, so they turned to me. During those six months, the battles were many, but nothing prepared me for the night of the vote. It seemed that not everyone wanted me to be the pastor. The church was split whether to place me as pastor. I learned this later. I truly believe that God put me in the position of pastor. All the battles from my previous experiences had given me and wife thick spiritual skin. I am not saying that I never struggle with my call. I would be lying if I said otherwise, but I would not trade these people and this church for the world. When I took over as pastor, we lost over half of our congregation in the next three years. Some that I thought would leave the church stayed. Those who I thought would stay left and went to other churches. I know that everything that I have told you is long and drawn out. It is important for the servant of Jesus Christ through the power of the Holy Spirit that you must stand strong in your faith because despite the intense battles, the war is won through Christ Jesus. The point is that Satan comes into the church through those whom you would never suspect. He destroys the church through subtle suggestion and obvious attacks to the core of congregations causing bitterness and dissension among the believers. I am working in the Lord Jesus with the Holy Spirit as my strength to encourage growth in the church I pastor. We have good days and not so good days, but God is good all the time!

> *'None of you shall approach anyone who is near of kin to him, to uncover his nakedness: I am the LORD.* **(Leviticus 18:6)**

> *You shall not lie with a male as with a woman. It is an abomination.* **(Leviticus 18:22)**

When our pastor left under questionable circumstances and I accepted the mantle as pastor, we lost over half of our congregation in the next three years. Some that I thought would leave the church stayed. Those who I thought would stay left and went to other churches. I know that everything that I have told you is long and drawn out. It is important for the servant of Jesus Christ through the power of the Holy Spirit that you must stand strong in your faith because despite the intense battles, the war is won through Christ Jesus. The point is that Satan comes into the church through those whom you would never suspect. He destroys the church through subtle suggestion and obvious attacks to the core of congregations causing bitterness and dissension among the believers. I am working in the Lord Jesus with the Holy Spirit as my strength to encourage growth in the church I pastor. We have good days and not so good days, but God is good all the time!

> **For this reason God gave them up to vile passions. For even their women exchanged the natural use for what is against nature. Likewise also the men, leaving the natural use of the woman, burned in their lust for one another, men with men committing what is shameful, and receiving in themselves the penalty of their error which was due. (Romans 1:26-27).**

The Christian church today is swallowed up in compromise and tolerance to the point there is no room for the truth of the gospel. The conflicts of the church are found in the many battles within Christianity globally. All of the various precepts that were the cornerstone of the believers in Jesus Christ in the first century have gradually been taken apart and given the lable "acceptable." The worldly ideals that Jesus so fervently and passionately spoke against, are not only received, as Satan would have, but they are given positions of authority and influence.

For example, in the mainline First United Methodist church, they investigated the validity of their stance on sexuality, primarily homosexuality and same-sex marriages. Why? Because many churches in the west and mid-west wanted the freedom to perform same-sex marriages and to allow homosexuals to be pastors of congregations and leaders in the churches? Is there not anyone out there who sees that this is wrong? Yes, we as Christians are not bound by the Mosaic laws, but we are to stand by God's laws of nature. If you going back to creation and the natural creation of all and you believe that Jesus Christ, the Word, was there and responsible for the creation of all (John 1:1-3), then you must know that He did not create (or speak into existence) two of the same gender.

God came to Sodom and Gomorrah, and at the pleading of Abraham, still only spared his immediate family who lived in Sodom. The men of Sodom said specifically that they wanted the men to come out so they could have sex with them. Because of their sexual immorality, they brought the fire from heaven down and utterly destroyed all the inhabitants within the cities of the plain. Why do we desire to tempt God in our lives? Satan knows the weaknesses and he exploits them to our own destruction. Do you not know that you are sealing your eternal destruction when partake in these diverse types of lifestyle?

> *"But whoever causes one of these little ones who believe in Me to stumble, it would be better for him if a millstone were hung around his neck, and he were thrown into the sea. If your hand causes you to sin, cut it off. It is better for you to enter into life maimed, rather than having two hands, to go to hell, into the fire that shall never be quenched— where*
> *'Their worm does not die*
> *And the fire is not quenched.'"* **(Mark 9:42-44)**

Another example of sexual immorality in the churches of Christianity is found in the Catholic church. Countless priests and leaders within the churches have been sexually abusing children in the house of God. This is an abomination and is not being addressed adequately as per the laws spelled out in the scripture. Many times in modern Christianity, there are those who think that they can lead two distinct but separate lives and still remain faithful to Jesus Christ. This is a lie from the devil himself. Jesus said,

> *"A disciple is not above his teacher, nor a servant above his master. It is enough for a disciple that he be like his teacher, and a servant like his master. If they have called the master of the house Beelzebub, how much more will they call those of his household! Therefore do not fear them. For there is nothing covered that will not be revealed, and hidden that*

will not be known. Whatever I tell you in the dark, speak in the light; and what you hear in the ear, preach on the housetops." **(Matthew 10:24-27)**

When the church refuses to accept Jesus' teachings on wealth, such as in Matthew 19:16-30, and approves of multi-million-dollar mansions and private jets for pastors, there is a real problem. Mainline denominations are taking the same authoritative path that the catholic church took in the sixteenth century when Martin Luther decided to rebel against the authority of the church and the Protestant Reformation began. Since then, the protestant movement has been fracturing over doctrinal disagreements because of denominational pride. The Catholic church of Martin Luther's day held the power both politically and religiously. This gave rise to the same problems that were being addressed by Jesus in His ministry. Therefore, Luther and many others rebelled and sought to worship a loving God because of His grace and mercy. Fear was the order of worship in the Catholic church. Any other way was blaspheming the Lord Jesus. In the following passages from the book of Revelation, we see clearly much of problems present in the churches today. The Lord Jesus is not pleased with the status of the churches and He is working to keep the church from falling deep into despair and the trappings of sin. The Satan knows that if he can enter the churches then he can defeat the Christian. Usually, they will invite him into the sanctuary, many times preaching and teaching a pseudo-gospel that draws everyone in for the kill.

The church today has festering sores that are cancerous because of the Christians today are complacent and tolerant of anything, even the abominations of scripture. In the church we find clergy abusing their positions of power and having adulterous relationships with parishioners commonplace, and when such clergy are criticised for it, the condemnation often falls not on the clergyman but on those criticising this behaviour, often the person who has been most wronged by the action. Both adultery and abuse of power are clearly stated to be wrong in scripture, but it seems some churches think their pastor's reputation is more important than that.

> *And even as they did not like to retain God in their knowledge, God gave them over to a debased mind, to do those things which are not fitting; being filled with all unrighteousness, sexual immorality, wickedness, covetousness, maliciousness; full of envy, murder, strife, deceit, evil-mindedness; they are whisperers, backbiters, haters of God, violent, proud, boasters, inventors of evil things, disobedient to parents, undiscerning, untrustworthy, unloving, unforgiving, unmerciful; who, knowing the righteous judgment of God, that those who practice such things are deserving of death, not only do the same but also approve of those who practice them.* **(Romans 1:28-32)**

The Apostle Paul, in writing these bold statements concerning the evil in his world, was prophetically declaring far worst times today. As we look at the Millennials and their society, it becomes more apparent that the world has fallen under the vile rule of the adversary, Satan. The church, in most of these ways, is reflecting the world and not Christ as the bride of Christ. When sexual immorality, envy, pride, covetousness, unforgiving, untrustworthy, and all the above are found in the churches, and especially the pulpit, it is on a steep decline into hell. This slippery slope has been growing more and more evident for the last nineteen hundred years. Satan has been invited into the churches and has taken residence its members.

The lines of right and wrong have been blurred to the point that the church has lost touch of the mission, vision, and purpose of its existence. We as the church stand back and watch as the church eats herself alive from the inside out. It is time for the people of God, those who truly love and desire the ways of God the Father, His Son Jesus Christ through the power of the Holy Spirit, to stand and fight against those who do not seek the righteousness and truth of God! Why? Because this is who we are called to be and what we are called to do! If we stand by idly and watch as the church,

God's people, the body of Christ rapidly fallen into the hands of the enemy, then we will be counted with the enemy. When we look at the despicable and heinous acts of child molesters, there should be no question as to the consequences of the crimes. In even the prisons today, they are many times sought after and killed for their actions. Sexual crimes in the world's eyes are evil, then how much more should they be in the eyes of the Christian and the church?

Christianity is not what you want it to be, it is how God designed it! His only Son came and died so that you would have eternal life. This is not the way to eternal life! The scriptures are just as real today as it was in the days of Jesus. Some churches are allowing pedophiles to work with children. Are the priests and preachers immune from the sin that is devastating the churches? The battles are real and the modern media is drawn to it like a tiger to a juicy slab of red meat. Today's media does not look for the positive near as much but seeks out the negative when it concerns the church. They are like rabid wolves. This is Satan in his attempted at destroying the testimony of the true church. Thousands of Christians around the world are executed for their beliefs. Are we ready to give account of our faith? Consider the seven churches of Revelation, but let's look hard at the selected of those churches and see where you and your church are found within them.

THE EPHESIAN CHURCH:

> *"I know your works, your labor, your patience, and that you cannot bear those who are evil. And you have tested those who say they are apostles and are not, and have found them liars; and you have persevered and have patience, and have labored for My name's sake and have not become weary.* **(Revelation 2:2-3)**

The church in Ephesus was a truly gifted congregation. They were the first church in the region of Asia Minor from which all others came. Notice how Jesus describes this church. As you look at the description, can you see your church resembling this church?

They were a very good and loving church toward the needy and are focused in their beliefs to the point of standing up against those who corrupt the gospel. Their endurance in the faith and perseverance is unmatched. They are sensitive to the Spirit in discerning false teachers and doctrine. You are thinking, why are they reprimanded? They lost sight of their true purpose and their first calling. They forgot the first pure love and faith in Christ Jesus that was in the beginning of their relationship with Him.

> ***Nevertheless I have this against you, that you have left your first love. Remember therefore from where you have fallen; repent and do the first works, or else I will come to you quickly and remove your lampstand from its place—unless you repent.* (Revelation 2:4-5)**

The only thing that the Lord Jesus has against this congregation is that they have lost their first love. What does this mean? If you look at the list of accomplishments the Lord spoke concerning this church, you would assume that the good would outweigh the bad. Right? God the Father, the Son, and the Holy Spirit has given you everything. He should expect no less from those who serve Him. This congregation, even though they were focused in their service, had lost sight of the real foundation of their faith. This is the reason He told them to go back to the beginning. The church was so involved in the service of others and concentrating on whether the others were following right doctrine that they lost sight of the true focus of their faith. Love, not condemnation, was to be the true call for service. Do not lose sight of the true faith in Jesus. This is where your first love rests, reside there and seek first the kingdom of God. Many pastors and leaders within the church lose sight of the call of God because they have forgotten what the love of the Lord was truly experienced in their lives. Therefore, they begin to stray away from the faith. When this happens, they look to the world for acceptance and love and not the Lord. When the leadership begins to lose its way, the congregation will soon follow.

THE CHURCH IN PERGAMOS:

> *But I have a few things against you, because you have there those who hold the doctrine of Balaam, who taught Balak to put a stumbling block before the children of Israel, to eat things sacrificed to idols, and to commit sexual immorality. Thus you also have those who hold the doctrine of the Nicolaitans, which thing I hate.* **(Revelation 2:14-15)**

Is there not a church like the one in Pergamos? The church was one of tolerance and compromise. They did not follow in the teachings of the Apostles and Jesus. Everything that the Apostle Paul had preached against, they were living and teaching to others. There is really nothing worse than a church that condones acceptance of the things causing obstacles for those who wish to follow the Lord Jesus. How can they call themselves Christians? Many churches cloak themselves under the guise of a Christian congregation but are only social clubs and fellowship groups for their own gain. The Lord said that they among those do the things that He hates and serves themselves rather than the interests of others.

> *Repent, or else I will come to you quickly and will fight against them with the sword of My mouth.* **(Revelation 2:16)**

The option here is an ultimatum for the church at Pergamos. Look around your congregation and pray that the Lord is not giving you the ultimatum. The option is not just to close the doors of the church, but whether to truly have the hope eternal. As we consider the possibility of the Christian church in crisis, it needs to be understood that even though you think that your church is strong and in line with the teachings of the gospel, they could be going down the path to destruction. So, repent and look to the Lord Jesus and His Holy Spirit fort guidance in your congregation. As you can see, the conflict in the church is real, even today. Look around and do not be blinded to the adversary in your churches.

The Church in Thyatira:

> *"I know your works, love, service, faith, and your patience; and as for your works, the last are more than the first."* **(Revelation 2:19)**

The church in Thyatira followed the teachings of the Lord. They were also humble in many ways. This is a common attribute of an active congregation. The problem comes when the church becomes corrupt in the manner of the business of the church. The example of this is the church I mentioned earlier from central Florida. The bottom line was more important than bringing souls into the kingdom of God. They were not concerned with the church as a place for the sinners to come and repent and learn how to grow closer to the risen Christ. The Lord knows everything the church does for Him and against Him. So, in many churches, they believe the Lord does not know what is done in secret. The Lord Himself said that all things done in the darkness will be brought into the light. The conflict to be found in these churches is shown in the following:

> ***Nevertheless I have a few things against you, because you allow that woman Jezebel, who calls herself a prophetess, to teach and seduce My servants to commit sexual immorality and eat things sacrificed to idols. And I gave her time to repent of her sexual immorality, and she did not repent. Indeed I will cast her into a sickbed, and those who commit adultery with her into great tribulation, unless they repent of their deeds. I will kill her children with death, and all the churches shall know that I am He who searches the minds and hearts. And I will give to each one of you according to your works.*** **(Revelation 2:20-23)**

The following of false teachings is as bad as those who teach it. There will be those who will come and say, "I am the Christ!" but they are wolves in sheep's clothing. Consider the cult followings of Reverend Jim Jones, Jonestown Massacre, and the People's church or even David Koresh and the Branch Davidians. There are people today who remain faithful followers of both. There are many more cults and sects that fall under this type of church. The followers believe that the leader or pastor is a messiah figure to them, and they will follow them to death. Is your church following the path of Jezebel? When Jesus tells His disciples that narrow is the way that leads to eternal life and broad is the way that leads to destruction, He is speaking to those who claim to believe but are deceived. Those who realize the wrong in all this and repent there is reward for them, but they must truly repent.

> *"Now to you I say, and to the rest in Thyatira, as many as do not have this doctrine, who have not known the depths of Satan, as they say, I will put on you no other burden. But hold fast what you have till I come. And he who overcomes, and keeps My works until the end, to him I will give power over the nations—*
> *'He shall rule them with a rod of iron; They shall be dashed to pieces like the potter's vessels'—*
> *as I also have received from My Father; and I will give him the morning star."* **(Revelation 2:24-28)**

The reward is great for those who understand something clearly at last of the true Christ and follow it. Jesus told His disciples that they must be discerning and know that the one they follow is the one who is true to scripture and true to the Father who is heaven. The reward for those who truly follow Christ as their Lord, they will be given the power to rule over the nations. Those who choose the path of destruction and follow the leader or pastor are rapidly going down a path to destruction and they will be dashed to pieces like the potter's vessel. This is not a group I am anxious to conform to and follow to death. Pastors and leaders are not perfect. They are not messiahs! So, we need to remove them from the pedestal and look to the Lord Jesus and His teachings.

The Church in Sardis:

> *"I know your works, that you have a name that you are alive, but you are dead. Be watchful, and strengthen the things which remain, that are ready to die, for I have not found your works perfect before God. Remember therefore how you have received and heard; hold fast and repent. Therefore if you will not watch, I will come upon you as a thief, and you will not know what hour I will come upon you."* **(Revelation 3:1-3)**

Jesus told them that they were a dead congregation. What do you think qualifies a congregation as dead? Do you believe that your congregation is dead? Why? Why not? In many churches today, there is a lack of understanding concerning what is a dead church. You do not have to put a lock on the doors to be dead. The congregation you are a part of can be active in all areas of ministry, but, they are just going through the motions. Are your people searching for ministries to get involved in? Is there a growing passion for serving the Lord Jesus or does it appear there is a quota or agenda being met? I have walked through the doors of churches that are active in every venue of ministry, yet there is no passion or even compassion. If these things you see in your congregation, then there needs to be true repentance. The problem is found in the fact that they are usually unaware that a problem exists. We think that we have all the time in the world, but tomorrow is not guaranteed for anyone. Only God knows the time, so repent.

> *"You have a few names even in Sardis who have not defiled their garments; and they shall walk with Me in white, for they are worthy. He who overcomes shall be clothed in white garments, and I will not blot out his name from the Book of Life; but I will confess his name before My Father and before His angels."* **(Revelation 3:4-5)**

In these churches, the Lord Jesus Christ gives an out or a chance to repent. Can you imagine, the Lord gives us so many chances, yet we always want one more chance to do the right thing.

The Battle for Eternity 41

He said that there were some in the church in Sardis that have not defiled their garments and are considered worthy. Their names will not be blotted out of the Book of Life. This implies that those who do not see their dead ways and repent, their names will be blotted out from the Book of Life. This tells us that they were once in the Book but now they are being removed. This does seem to make one reconsider the whole notion of once saved always saved. The churches of today look to their doctrines and not to the scriptures for their truths. The truth is in the gospel of Jesus Christ and no other. Doctrines and theologies are created by man and discussed in conference rooms where the arguments over one-ply or two-ply toilet paper cause churches to divide. People often ask me why there are so many different churches. In the small town in southern Alabama that I grew up in, population of about two thousand people, there were thirty-seven churches in a ten-mile radius. Now, if you consider that these churches on average have no more than twelve to thirty people in them, and, that on average, about half of them are not aware of their salvation, then we should be severely dissatisfied with the job that we are doing for the Lord. Sure, most of the two thousand can say that they go to church. But does that make them Christians and faithful followers of Christ as we have been called to be? Jesus said that if you confess Him before men then He will confess you before His Father in heaven and the angels. Wow! What an assurance, but we need to do our part! Stop being a dead church! Come back to the life of the gospel!

THE CHURCH IN LAODICEA:

> *"I know your works, that you are neither cold nor hot. I could wish you were cold or hot. So then, because you are lukewarm, and neither cold nor hot, I will vomit you out of My mouth. Because you say, 'I am rich, have become wealthy, and have need of nothing'—and do not know that you are wretched, miserable, poor, blind, and naked."*
> **(Revelation 3:15-17)**

The greatest aspect of the conflict that strikes within the churches is that they are blind to the sin that stares them in their faces. They do not want to believe that they fall short of the glory of God, but this is the ones whom the Lord abhors the most because they are not consistent in their faith. What they believe is not how they act. Whichever way the wind blows is the direction they move. Right or wrong, they follow those who are popular or rich or famous. They are following those who will help grow the church in number, not souls. They look at the bottom line and not at the standard line set by Christ. Jesus said that He wishes that they would be either hot or cold, but because they lukewarm, He will vomit you up out of His mouth. What a visual! I do not want to make Jesus sick to even look at me. Among these are those churches who are "self-sufficient" in that they are doing fine without God. God and morals just complicate things, right?

The churches mentioned are just for reflection. But Jesus showed these churches to John for him show them the error of their ways, so they could have opportunity to repent. The churches of Smyrna and Philadelphia are not mentioned here because they were following the commands of the Lord and setting the example for the others to follow. He shows these seven churches to John, so he could give the churches examples of the right and wrong ways of serving the Lord Jesus. In the conflict, as you can see, there is no safe place in the world apart from the Lord Jesus Christ. He is our refuge and strength. As I have stressed before, the war is real and the daily battles are real, so be ready to armor up and sharpen your sword and be ready in season and out of season to give an account of the testimony of your faith. May the Lord Jesus Christ be praised in all you say and do, Amen!

3

THE ENEMIES OF YOUR SOUL

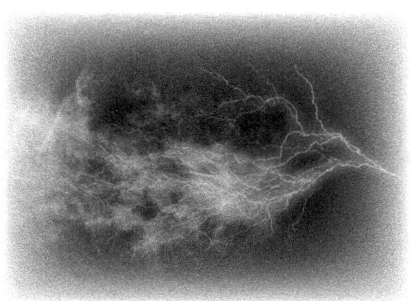

> *For we do not wrestle against flesh and blood, but against principalities, against powers, against the rulers of the darkness of this age, against spiritual hosts of wickedness in the heavenly places. Therefore take up the whole armor of God, that you may be able to withstand in the evil day, and having done all, to stand.* **(Ephesians 6:12-13)**

The first thing that you think of when an enemy is mentioned, in your spiritual life, is Satan or the fallen angel Lucifer. We cannot blame everything that goes wrong in our lives on Satan. We need to take some credit on our own. The truth is that we are our worst enemies. But, for the sake of argument for the battle for eternity, we are looking at all aspects of those things that tend to hinder and even turn us away from an acting faith in Jesus Christ. In this chapter, we will study the overwhelming Biblical understanding of the enemies that torment us in our walk with Christ daily.

The understanding of spiritual warfare in the life of the Christian is fought on two fronts. The Christian, believe it or not, is more open to spiritual conflict than most in the world. Those who are bound by the ways of the world are given to everything that the world offers. To understand the battle, you must first approach the subject of the enemy. Yes! The adversary, the devil, Satan, Lucifer, is the enemy. Then, why do we say that we are our own worst enemy? Because we are the worst enemy that we encounter. Why? We are given the tools with prayer, holy scripture, and spiritual examples to help guide us down the right path and do the right thing. But, we, as humans with a human nature that is flawed and tainted, must make the conscious choice to do or say the right thing. Unfortunately, the sinful nature dictates for us to naturally choose the wrong action most of the time on our own.

The battles, and the ultimate war that is raging, is a spiritual one. You as a child of the living God have the power, through the power and authority of the Holy Spirit, to defeat the enemy in any conflict. But, you must believe and let the Spirit of God work in you and through you. Jesus looked to the Father for everything in His life and ministry. Are we any different? Should we be different? No! Jesus was the example that God the Father sent to demonstrate to us how to live a godly life. Not only that, but, when God the Father sent the Son, He gave us a "how to" manual in the holy scriptures as to how to defeat the enemy, even the enemy within us. Jesus did not just come and live as a human just to come "hang out" with us. He came to experience every emotion, pain, hunger, sickness, anguish, hurt that we experience in a lifetime. But He also came to show us how to experience true joy, love, mercy, compassion, grace, humility, and forgiveness, because humans are not capable of true love, mercy and compassion as shown by God. We are unable to grasp this concept and employ them into our lives.

The war is raging around us constantly. If you could see the battle, you would run and hide in a dark corner. The problem with this is that the battles are never ceasing, and they are fighting for your soul. If this is true, then should you not be willing to stand firm and fight on the front lines of the war? You have everything at stake. Jesus said that we should not fear the ones who can destroy the body, but we should fear the one who can destroy both body and soul. The adversary cannot take your soul unless you willingly give it up to him. So, why do we, for a moment of pleasure, give up our soul for an eternity of anguish? In the present society in which we live, patience is no longer a virtue. In fact, our natures today, directed by the media, internet, and a self-driven, self-achieving world, determine that patience is obsolete. We want results and we want them now! So, yes, we are our worst enemy in life. The Christian does not believe they need to focus on the goal because the goal has already been determined for us. The results of the prayers are to be given now. I must have a new car now! I must have the perfect job, house, car, boat, spouse, and children now! We should not have to work for our eternal hope. Why do you believe that you are any different than The Apostle Paul, Moses, John the Baptist, even Jesus? Every day is a battle for eternity. Are you armed and ready for battle? If you are not ready, then you need to fear the one who will destroy both body and soul, because he will do it!

SATAN: BLINDS PEOPLE TO THE TRUTH

> *But we have renounced the hidden things of shame, not walking in craftiness nor handling the word of God deceitfully, but by manifestation of the truth commending ourselves to every man's conscience in the sight of God. But even if our gospel is veiled, it is veiled to those who are perishing, whose minds the god of this age has blinded, who do not believe, lest the light of the gospel of the glory of Christ, who is the image of God, should shine on them.* **(2 Corinthians 4:2-4)**

The god of this age is none other than Satan himself. The greatest deception of this fallen angel is for everyone to believe that he does not exist. Much of the world and even much of the church seem to believe that we live in hell now and there is only heaven beyond this age. A truly deceitful twisting of the Word of God. There are many who believe that the god of this world is more powerful and will defeat the God of all. You see, Satan will blind you to the truth and lead you down the wide path to destruction. Jesus told His disciples that in the last days even the elite will be deceived. The Apostle Paul was dealing with a very religiously deceived church in Corinth. The more he encouraged them, the more they would falter. He said that even if the gospel was veiled or withdrawn from the understanding of all but those chosen few, the light of the gospel of Christ will shine into the darkness of the god of the age. Truth, God's Truth, can only set you free from sin and death. Satan's deceptions are poured out for one purpose and that is the destruction of all humanity.

How has he blinded the people of God? It is through the twisting of the Word of God. At the garden with Adam and Eve, for example, he took God's own words that He spoke to Adam and twisted them on Eve. Why did he focus on the woman? Because God had given the command directly to Adam and then he relayed it her. Not fully understanding the implications and consequences of the act, she had no reason not to believe the serpent. The serpent was creation of God too. Satan, the adversary, also deceived humanity from the time of Adam's first son Cain. He deceived him into bringing and inadequate offering to Him. God gave precise instructions and why He wanted the offerings to be that way and Cain did not follow it. Jealousy, pride and envy raged as God rejected his offering, Cain believed and followed the deception of the deceiver and killed his brother. David, a man after God's own heart, followed the wiles of deception and committed adultery, treachery, and murder. But when Nathan called his attention to his sins, he repented, but not without consequences. You see, the deceiver, Satan, can offer you the desires of your heart, but a twisted version and with consequences, eternal in intent.

He, Satan, Lucifer, the fallen one, has even deceived the church today by the overwhelming sin of compromise and tolerance. Many denominations have accepted clergy sexually abusing choir members and members of youth groups and instead of informing the police, have moved those clergy on to another church or parish, leaving them still holding positions of power and authority over God's people.

What is wrong with this picture?! Why do we even have to ask that question? What is right with it?

> *At that time the disciples came to Jesus, saying, "Who then is greatest in the kingdom of heaven?"*
> *Then Jesus called a little child to Him, set him in the midst of them, and said, "Assuredly, I say to you, unless you*

are converted and become as little children, you will by no means enter the kingdom of heaven. Therefore whoever humbles himself as this little child is the greatest in the kingdom of heaven. Whoever receives one little child like this in My name receives Me." **(Matthew 18:1-5)**

The light of life is found in each child. If you have ever just been present for the birth of a child and witnessed the innocence of that child, then why would you who are not evil choose to do evil to one of these. This is an unspeakable act against a true innocent of God's most beautiful of God's creations. All the acts against children born and unborn are atrocities against God and humanity. Childhood sexual abuse, Abortion, and childhood abuse in any form, why am I putting these together into one category? Because they all represent murder. The death of innocence where the victim has no recourse and they are defenseless. Why are there those in the churches who abuse children for their own perverted pleasure? Because Satan, the adversary, has been allowed. The people of God are just sitting back in the pews and allowing this to take place!

So Jesus said, "Are you also still without understanding? Do you not yet understand that whatever enters the mouth goes into the stomach and is eliminated? But those things which proceed out of the mouth come from the heart, and they defile a man. For out of the heart proceed evil thoughts, murders, adulteries, fornications, thefts, false witness, blasphemies. These are the things which defile a man, but to eat with unwashed hands does not defile a man." **(Matthew 15:16-20)**

Jesus spoke to His disciples very frankly concerning what is considered defilement. The heart is where all actions proceed from toward others. Do we understand the perverted pleasure one person has for another? No, but that does not make it good! The world develops sciences devoted to the study and attempted understanding of perverse and evil mind and heart. Jesus says here plainly when speaking with His disciples, that it is from the heart where your true love flows and a person commits adultery, murder, incest, and any other form of sexual immorality is an abomination before God. Because of the fallen sinful nature of humanity, we have to make a conscious effort to repent and completely change our minds and hearts toward Jesus Christ as our Savior and Lord.

THE ENEMY ALLOWED TO ATTACK WITH LIMITS

> *Then the LORD said to Satan, "Have you considered My servant Job, that there is none like him on the earth, a blameless and upright man, one who fears God and shuns evil?"*
>
> *So Satan answered the LORD and said, "Does Job fear God for nothing? Have You not made a hedge around him, around his household, and around all that he has on every side? You have blessed the work of his hands, and his possessions have increased in the land. But now, stretch out Your hand and touch all that he has, and he will surely curse You to Your face!"*
>
> *And the LORD said to Satan, "Behold, all that he has is in your power; only do not lay a hand on his person."*
>
> *So Satan went out from the presence of the LORD.* **(Job 1:8-12)**

The greatest deception of Satan is the belief that he does not exist. But God has control over the actions of Satan and his attacks. Does God enjoy our suffering at the hand of His immortal enemy? No! Absolutely not! Satan approaches God testing Him. God, being omnipotent, knows the heart of Job and the intent of Satan. He wants to show the adversary that humanity is a worthwhile cause and more resilient than he gives them credit for. God tells him the list of the characteristics that Job possesses. He tells Satan if he is wanting to attack Job and destroy his credibility, then he should consider that he is a most righteous man. God told him that Job was His greatest servant. He was an upright and blameless man in whom there was no fault. Also, He said that Job is a man who fears God and shuns evil. This is to entice Satan to a challenge, knowing

The Battle for Eternity

he will lose. God knows Satan's intent, it is the same every time he comes into the presence of God and the Sons of God. The attacks are aimed to the destruction of all that is precious to God. This is to humiliate God and to attempt to show that God is not all powerful.

Satan then answers God with the classic response. He asks an interesting question. "Does Job fear God for nothing?" Consider this for a moment and look at the description of Job given by God. God saw Job in an endearing light. He had great confidence in Job and his faith in God. God knew that regardless of what loss Satan had prepared for Job that he would remain faithful. But, Satan has apparently considered Job and has probably made attempts to get to him. Because, he says that God has a hedge of protection around him. Do you believe that God has a hedge of protection around each of us? The battle for our soul is not one taken lightly by God. He is with us in His Son Jesus Christ. When you give your life to Jesus Christ, He protects and helps you grow in faith and love for Him in all things. We are His children engrafted into the family of God through His Son Jesus Christ in the power of the Holy Spirit. Jesus is there always to protect us against the attacks of the enemy. Our hedge of protection is described in Ephesians by the Apostle Paul as the "Full Armor of God." This we will discuss in the next chapter. But, for this study, we must believe in the fact that regardless to how bad it truly gets that God is in control and He has that hedge of protection around us.

He also notices that not only does God have a hedge around and blesses everything he does, but He has a hedge around and blesses his family, household, and all he possesses. Anything Job has and does is blessed because of his faithfulness and dedication to God. God did not just randomly select Job for this purpose. There was an eternally pointed purpose. Satan believes that humanity is so depraved and lost in their sin that it would not take but a slight push in the right direction to make them curse God and turn away. Satan, in his conniving, deceptiveness, saw a clear opportunity to show God's vulnerability and lack of knowledge of those who serve Him. He took the hook! He told God that if He would reach out

His hand and touch all that he has then he will curse God to His face. God told him, "Alright, all that he has is in your power." In other words, God told him to do his worst. But, the only condition that God sets for Satan was that he was not to touch his person. Satan, I am sure, thought that he had this one won. God sets limits on the attacks we receive by the adversary. Why then does God even allow us to be attacked? Because, in our deepest moments, as we look to Him for our strength, we are strengthened in our faith. Instead of growing weaker, we grow in our faith and our resolve becomes more steadfast and our stand in the faith, firmer.

The first century church was a classic example of the attacks of the adversary working against the intent of God. The Holy Spirit was given to the disciples on the day of Pentecost in Acts chapter two. This was truly a world defining event in creation. Satan knew he had failed at destroying the Son of God. He then turned to those whom He had taught and given the knowledge of God. The disciples were given power from on high. The interesting part in this is that it had to have been a slap in the face of the adversary. Because, in his pride, he believed that he was entitled to that power, but God chose to give that power and the opportunity to be sons and daughters of God, to humanity. He lifted humanity and gave them power over Satan and his forces. So, you see that nothing can come against you, if you humble yourself, pray, seek His face and turn from your wicked ways and follow Him in all things. Look to the example of Job and his faith. The actions of Job were predicted and anticipated by Satan when he approached God in heaven. God knew that Job's faithfulness would overcome adversity and loss. Job was focused in all things on God and righteousness was accredited to him by God because of this devotion and commitment. He knew that God was there in the good and the bad, why Christians today are oblivious to this is troubling for the church.

> ***Then the Lord said to Satan, "Have you considered My servant Job, that there is none like him on the earth, a blameless and upright man, one who fears God and shuns***

> *evil? And still he holds fast to his integrity, although you incited Me against him, to destroy him without cause."*
>
> *So Satan answered the L**ORD** and said, "Skin for skin! Yes, all that a man has he will give for his life. But stretch out Your hand now, and touch his bone and his flesh, and he will surely curse You to Your face!"*
>
> *And the L**ORD** said to Satan, "Behold, he is in your hand, but spare his life."* **(Job 2:3-6)**

This time Satan could attack Job's body to further prove the point that humans were not capable of faith and love for God. The picture that is given here is that of "I told you so." This incites Satan even more because God tells him despite him being attacked, he "holds fast to his integrity, although you incited Me against him." Satan's response was interesting because it spoke to the selfish concerns of the human nature. If a person is truly focused and dependent on God in all things, then his own body is last on the list of concerns. They are more concerned about the welfare and survival of others. Satan's lack of understanding when it comes to the nature of the human as a lover of God is astonishing. He was cast out of heaven because of the very reason that he attacked Job. The key is found in the tag that God sets for Satan. Despite the allowance to attack, it comes with limitations. In all things, he was never allowed to take his life. Job's soul belonged to God.

The amusing portion of this story is that Satan did not kill or do anything to Job's wife. I believe that he prompted her to come against her husband as another added insult to injury. He could destroy Job's possessions and kill his family except for his wife. Her response is classic for a wife who has gone through as much as she has and witnessed as much as she has witnessed. The statement seems harsh, but it is a response out of a lack of understanding. ***Then his wife said to him, "Do you still hold fast to your integrity? Curse God and die!"*** **(Job 2:9)** She does not understand what is happening to them. It is not just to Job, but to her as well. Satan allowed her to remain whole, but it was more difficult for Job that she lacked support for him and his faith. We find this mentality in the Christian who is weak in their faith even today in the church.

> *But he said to her, "You speak as one of the foolish women speaks. Shall we indeed accept good from God, and shall we not accept adversity?" In all this Job did not sin with his lips.* **(Job 2:10)**

When Job speaks, we need to take note and learn from his faith. Look at the church today and the society in which we live. Do you seek God's good apart from chastisement? Do we only accept the good and not the bad? God allows the trials and tribulations to come our way, not because He loves to torture. He allows these things to come into our lives to strengthen our faith. The more our faith is strengthened, the closer we grow into that intimate relationship God wants to have with us. The great statement that truly sets the stage for the remainder of this story is that "in all this Job did not sin with his lips". Wow! What a testimony for the Christian today. If God is for us who can be against us for we have an advocate with the Father, Jesus the Son of God. Job's faith may have skipped a beat in his heart, but he did not speak against the Lord God. Remember, Satan is only allowed to do certain things against you. This is the promise of Christ Jesus that you will be persecuted, even to the point of death, but you are the only one who can release your soul to the enemy. Stand firm, because your faith and salvation are what holds you between eternal life and death!

THE COMMON ENEMY AND THE DEFENSE

> *But sanctify the Lord God in your hearts, and always be ready to give a defense to everyone who asks you a reason for the hope that is in you, with meekness and fear; having a good conscience, that when they defame you as evildoers, those who revile your good conduct in Christ may be ashamed.* **(1 Peter 3:15-16)**

We must realize, as Christians, that we are called to sanctify ourselves before a Holy and Just God. But, Peter is calling for you to sanctify the Lord God in your hearts. This means that the Lord God, through Jesus Christ His Son, you can be made clean and presentable before a Holy God. Because God should destroy us all. But, He loves us so much! He continues and says that we should always be ready to give account and reason for the hope that we have and that is in us. We cannot stand against the enemy apart from the empowering of the Holy Spirit with the grace of God in our lives. To sanctify ourselves with the Lord Jesus Christ in our lives is a lifelong task that we are incapable of completing our mission without the work of the Holy Spirit and the grace of God.

He calls you, in all things, to have a good conscience. Why is this important? Peter says that you do this so those who attempt to call you an evil doer, though you do these things in Christ, they will be brought down and shamed. How many of you have encountered in the workplace such individuals? How about in your own family or in church? Why is this important for us as Christians? Because our greatest enemy is us. We are the one who either gives our life over to God and His love and grace or we succumb. This may be difficult to accept, but it is the reality. There will always be something or someone who will do or say something that hurts our little feelings, move forward and focus on Christ.

Sanctify yourselves in the Lord Jesus in your hearts. We should not be passive in our Christianity, but active and ready to give an account of the grace of God through Jesus Christ. Peter says that we must enter this relationship with fear, but also with meekness. How is your relationship with the Lord Jesus Christ? Is it only when you cross the threshold of the church sanctuary or is it every moment of everyday? Standing firm in the power of the Lord Jesus Christ and His love and those say and do evil against you will be ashamed. They will receive their reward in the end. This reminds me of the story of Jonah. Jonah was a zealot for the Lord God, but he truly did not see the big picture as God saw it. God called Jonah to go to Nineveh and bring them the message of repentance. Nineveh was noted to be a very powerful and influential city. Sin was rampant throughout the known world, but especially in Nineveh. Jonah was angry with God because He wanted to call the city to repentance. Jonah thought it was going to be a waste of time and he would die there. He was so adamant in his conviction that he ran the opposite direction. But God chose Jonah for a task for a reason. God was determined to have Jonah complete the task.

Jonah spoke evil against a people he did not know but knew about. God was equally setting out to demonstrate His love and mercy not only toward the people of Nineveh, but also toward Jonah. This story is just as much a story of Jonah's conviction and repentance as was the repentance of entire city. Peter was telling us this same story, but in a more contemporary context. He makes God's plan relevant in every situation. He was trying to show Jonah that regardless to how evil and sinful a people may be, God's purpose and plan will be fulfilled.

> ***Little children, let no one deceive you. He who practices righteousness is righteous, just as He is righteous. He who sins is of the devil, for the devil has sinned from the beginning. For this purpose the Son of God was manifested, that He might destroy the works of the devil. Whoever has been born of God does not sin, for His seed remains in him; and he cannot sin, because he has been born of God.* (1John 3:7-9)**

Jesus the Holy Son of God is the greatest defense we have in the battle for eternity. Satan has no foothold in the world that God created except what God allows and we concede to and accept. We have much more power over the evil one than we realize. The Bible tells us that the adversary stalks about looking for who he can devour. We have a responsibility as Christians to unite and strive to be focused on the race ahead. The Apostle John tells us that the whole reason for Jesus the Son of God to come and be manifested is to destroy the works of the devil. From the beginning, the devil destroyed the witnesses and testimonies of those who truly served the Lord God.

THE EVIL WORK OF SATAN: TEMPTATION

> *Now the serpent was more cunning than any beast of the field which the* LORD *God had made. And he said to the woman, "Has God indeed said, 'You shall not eat of every tree of the garden'?"*
> *And the woman said to the serpent, "We may eat the fruit of the trees of the garden; but of the fruit of the tree which is in the midst of the garden, God has said, 'You shall not eat it, nor shall you touch it, lest you die.'"*
> *Then the serpent said to the woman, "You will not surely die. For God knows that in the day you eat of it your eyes will be opened, and you will be like God, knowing good and evil."* **(Genesis 3:1-5)**

This is the first implication of Satan in scripture having to do with temptation though this does not specifically name Satan as the tempter. The belief, even elsewhere in scripture, points to him as the tempter. The way the serpent twists the words of the Lord God is a strong indicator that Satan was involved. This scene is vividly played out because of the innocence of the first of creation. Adam and Eve did not know or even understand the concept of sin or even the difference between good and evil. God knew their heart and their capability not to sin. This was their test of perfection. The consideration here should be that God even allowed Satan to tempt the first man and woman to test them with the one thing He trusted to them.

When the adversary tempts us, there is always a thread of truth that runs through the deception. If God tells us to do something, then the temptation of not doing it brings up many excuses. We tend to question the motives of God. Why does God really want me to visit this person or talk to this other person? Why do we question God? Do we know better than the Lord God Almighty? Looking back to Adam and Eve, it is difficult to associate our current condition with that of our first parents. Satan has worked the art of deception since the beginning in the garden. The innocence of the first couple was simple enough for the deception to take root in human nature. We know the truth of the Lord, yet we still follow the easy path. The problem is that the easy path toward worldly pleasures leads to the broad road of destruction.

THE EVIL WORK OF SATAN: SLANDERING THE SAINTS

> *So Satan answered the LORD and said, "Does Job fear God for nothing? Have You not made a hedge around him, around his household, and around all that he has on every side? You have blessed the work of his hands, and his possessions have increased in the land. But now, stretch out Your hand and touch all that he has, and he will surely curse You to Your face!"* **(Job 1:9-11)**

The deception of Satan is real in our lives. The problem is in our response to the deception. Regardless of how Satan attacked Job, he remained faithful. He stands before the throne of God as a prosecutor in a court room. In our case today, we live in the New Covenant with God through Jesus Christ. Jesus is our defense attorney and He has not lost a case yet. Praise God!

> *My little children, these things I write to you, so that you may not sin. And if anyone sins, we have an Advocate with the Father, Jesus Christ the righteous. And He Himself is the propitiation for our sins, and not for ours only but also for the whole world.* **(1 John 2:1-2)**

In 1John chapter two, Jesus is standing on our behalf before the Father. He is called the advocate or defense attorney who stands and fights on our behalf. As we see and comprehend the steadfastness of Job, we need to look deep into our own faith or lack of faith. In the end, we are our own worst enemy and Satan knows it and he uses this against the saints for their destruction. When Jesus taught on the Mount of Olives His first recorded sermon to the disciples, He made a point to direct the focus of their faith not just towards physical persecution. The defamation and slander of one's character leaves a much deeper scar throughout their life than any physical persecution or abuse.

> *"Blessed are you when they revile and persecute you, and say all kinds of evil against you falsely for My sake. Rejoice and be exceedingly glad, for great is your reward in heaven, for so they persecuted the prophets who were before you."* **(Matthew 5:11-12)**

If we truly believe that Jesus is the Son of God and that He truly defended us by dying on the cross, then there should not be any question concerning His faithfulness to us. We should realize that there were far more multitudes of saints that have endured before us and there will be more after us. Jesus never promised that the Christian life would be without persecution and trials. On the contrary, He specifically told His disciples that they will be persecuted because of Him. The most difficult part of being a Christian is growing a thick skin due to persecution. The wonderful thing concerning the Christian faith is that the more we endure from Satan and his temptations, the closer we can get to Jesus and knowing His as our Savior and Lord. Remember, though Satan may slander and defame you because of your faith, you will always have someone who loves you so much that He voluntarily gave Himself up to be tortured and gruesomely killed on the cross for you. You know what?! He would do it again. But we know that does not have to do it again because His sacrifice was enough for all, forever! Amen!

THE EVIL WORK OF SATAN: OPPOSING THE RIGHTEOUS

> *Then he showed me Joshua the high priest standing before the Angel of the LORD, and Satan standing at his right hand to oppose him. And the LORD said to Satan, "The LORD rebuke you, Satan! The LORD who has chosen Jerusalem rebuke you! Is this not a brand plucked from the fire?"* **(Zechariah 3:1-2)**

The works of the adversary are clear in the world and even in the churches. Satan never sleeps. He schemes every moment of every day in a relentless pursuit to destroy God and His precious creation. What we may think is trivial, the devil uses to turn back on us and God. Our greatest defense against such a determined foe is our testimony and our faith. This is even more evident than in the pastors who I served. They were righteous men of God who became complacent in their faith and fell into temptation. We, as Christians, need to be mindful of this trap. This is the easiest way that the adversary ensnares faithful people of the congregation of believers. I have not seen this more evident than in the church that I presently pastor. As I said in the previous chapter, the church was split and over half the congregation left. The judgment of those who left under questionable reasons is left to the Lord. The church was scared from the deception and destruction that wrought from those involved. The adversary will turn the body of Christ to devour itself. The greatest enemy of the church is found within itself. Be mindful of the wiles of the devil because he roaming about ready to destroy all who are precious to God the Father.

THE EVIL WORK OF SATAN: REMOVING THE GOOD SEED

> *Then He spoke many things to them in parables, saying: "Behold, a sower went out to sow. And as he sowed, some seed fell by the wayside; and the birds came and devoured them. Some fell on stony places, where they did not have much earth; and they immediately sprang up because they had no depth of earth. But when the sun was up they were scorched, and because they had no root they withered away. And some fell among thorns, and the thorns sprang up and choked them. But others fell on good ground and yielded a crop: some a hundredfold, some sixty, some thirty. He who has ears to hear, let him hear!"* **(Matthew 13:3-9)**

The Battle for Eternity 59

The good seed is the Word of God and it is spread as according to the husbandman, who is God the Father. We need to understand that as Christians we are not immune to the attacks of Satan. In fact, you will be persecuted for your faith in the gospel of Jesus Christ. He told His disciples from the beginning that the road to eternity in heaven is not an easy one. Jesus told them that they would suffer, even die for the faith. Most Christians today, in most parts of the United States, have not suffered true persecution. Satan attacks you when you are most vulnerable.

For example, Jesus said in His parable that a sower, you who share the gospel with someone, went out to sow seed, the word of God. The first portions of seed shared fell to the wayside. These, I believe, were those who were passing by as the word of God was being shared. They may have not been targeted, but they heard it. The problem was that as they heard it, they were directed by Satan in their thoughts with preconceived ideas of the message. They were not truly open or even ready for the reception of the truth. If they were nourished by Godly people, they could have been saved from the evil one. They gave into the worldly pleasures and succumbed to the ways of the world. They were easy prey for the evil pleasures of the world.

The next group was those to whom the first seeds were intended. These seeds were thrown among the stony places. They come into the church in droves. They are brought into the church and quickly made members. These individuals may be required to take a membership class. This is primarily for informational purposes. Because these people are not truly mentored, they will fall between the cracks and forgotten, unless they take initiative for themselves. Because their faith is weak and there is nobody to come along side of them and show them what it means to be a Christian, when the heat comes against them in some issue, their faith will wither and die. There is no root or foundation on which build that relationship that is so vital to daily personal and spiritual growth. These are easy prey, even though they are in the church, they will leave because of their lack of understanding and that no one will take time to love them and them.

THE EVIL WORK OF SATAN: SOWING THE WEEDS

> *Another parable He put forth to them, saying: "The kingdom of heaven is like a man who sowed good seed in his field; but while men slept, his enemy came and sowed tares among the wheat and went his way. But when the grain had sprouted and produced a crop, then the tares also appeared. So the servants of the owner came and said to him, 'Sir, did you not sow good seed in your field? How then does it have tares?' He said to them, 'An enemy has done this.' The servants said to him, 'Do you want us then to go and gather them up?' But he said, 'No, lest while you gather up the tares you also uproot the wheat with them. Let both grow together until the harvest, and at the time of harvest I will say to the reapers, "First gather together the tares and bind them in bundles to burn them, but gather the wheat into my barn."'"*
> **(Matthew 13:24-30)**

We know the strategy of the enemy in our lives. He seeks to do nothing but to steal, kill, and destroy. The key to defeating your enemy is to know them and study their ways. Only look at the history of humanity to see the attempts and failures of the enemy. He has tried and failed on many levels throughout the history of this marvelous planet. I told my son when he was going to bootcamp several years old that to defeat the opponent you must think at least three to five moves ahead of them. But, to think ahead of them you must first know them.

In the parable of the sower and the weeds, Jesus was telling His disciples a hard truth, but a realization concerning the personal struggles that will befall those who are faithful. The truth is that though the good seed fell upon us, the seed can be choked out by the weeds of the sinful world around us. In the end, these weeds will be sifted as chaff and cast into the eternal fire. In the meantime, the weeds are a means of strengthening for our faith and, for a lack

The Battle for Eternity

of a better term, unavoidable. This may be a difficult teaching for most to understand, but it is necessary for the strengthening of our faith. The weeds in our lives are there for us to look to Christ for our strength, power, and authority in life.

> ***Do not be deceived, God is not mocked; for whatever a man sows, that he will also reap. For he who sows to his flesh will of the flesh reap corruption, but he who sows to the Spirit will of the Spirit reap everlasting life.*** **(Galatians 6:7-8)**

The Christian must not give the enemy the edge in this eternal war. The advantage that Christians possess is that we are given the opportunity by God the Father to see the playbook of the opposing team. The word of God, the sword, is our greatest weapon. When the word of God is spoken, the devil flees. Why? Because the word of God is truth and he is the father of lies. Though Satan cannot make you do anything as a Christian, he can tempt you and nudge you in that direction to make you sin. You may not even realize the influences that the enemy has on you. Therefore, the Christian must arm themselves against the enemy with the word of God.

When spreading the seeds of the gospel of Christ, one must consider that the enemy is working even harder to destroy those seeds and turn them against God. This is the goal of the enemy. Remember that the seeds of the flesh reap corruption which leads to destruction and death eternal. But those who seek sow to please the Spirit of God reap eternal life. I am of the belief that those who seek to sow the seeds of the flesh are ignorant and lazy to the consequences of the flesh. It is immediate satisfaction which is the sinful nature. Those who seek after the Spirit of God are the ones who have walked away from the sinful nature and embraced the Holy Spirit of God as their strength and guiding light.

> ***A worthless person, a wicked man,***
> ***Walks with a perverse mouth;***
> ***He winks with his eyes,***
> ***He shuffles his feet,***
> ***He points with his fingers;***

> ***Perversity is in his heart,***
> ***He devises evil continually,***
> ***He sows discord.***
> ***Therefore his calamity shall come suddenly;***
> ***Suddenly he shall be broken without remedy.***
> **(Proverbs 6:12-15)**

    The enemy and the armies he has and will assemble are defeated. His goal is to drag as many of God's chosen into the lake of fire and brimstone with him as he can. Let us not give him the edge. We as Christians must fight to the death. This might sound medieval, but that is the war where we find ourselves in the midst. We must stand firm in our beliefs and in the word of God and His promises. The problem with most Christians today is that tolerance and contentedness has made the sharp edge of their verbal swords dull and rusty. In America, the only persecution is seen on television. There is so much of this seen in the news and movies that we become desensitized to the fact that sin is even dominating churches.

    The edge in this war for the souls of humanity is being handed over to the enemy. The churches are opening their doors and inviting the devil into their holy places and even allowing him into the pulpits today. As I say this, you may be appalled at the idea of this even being a consideration but look at the church today. The church has allowed prayer and the pledge of allegiance to be taken out of schools. The ten commandments to be removed from the court houses and public places. All this is because only a handful of people decided they were offended and Christians, who are millions strong, stand by and let it happen. This was the beginning of the decline of the household and family in America. Only recently have we seen an increase in Christians who are willing to stand up for those values that made us strongest in this fight from the beginning. It is time to take the upper ground back from the enemy! This Proverb is one for Christians to stand strong in the belief that we live in our Lord and should be more firm in our stance as we stand and fight against the weaker and broken-down enemy. Know the enemy and know him well because he knows you. Are ready and willing to stand and fight in the Name of the Father, the Son, and the Holy Spirit?!

4

Our Weapons

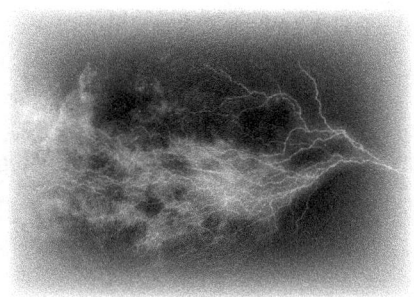

Then David said to the Philistine, "You come to me with a sword, with a spear, and with a javelin. But I come to you in the name of the L<small>ORD</small> of hosts, the God of the armies of Israel, whom you have defied.
(1 Samuel 17:45)

What are the weapons of the warfare of the soul? The Word of God! David, as a young shepherd boy did everything to protect no only the sheep in his care but his faith in the Lord God who sheltered and cared for him. When he saw the giant blaspheme the Lord God, David reacted to defend his God. What was the strongest weapon used by David? It was not the sling or the stone which he slung at Goliath. The strongest weapon in David's arsenal was his faith. He had no doubt in his mind that the Lord God would deliver him from the giant. If we stand strong and faithful for Him, then He will stand strong with us and for us in times of facing our giants.

Goliath came from a family of true giants who were Philistines. Among those who were listed as of the line of the Nephilim, Goliath and his brothers were from Gath. Gath was one of the cities not conquered during the conquest. It was also listed among the cities of the descendants of the Nephilim. Remember, the Nephilim were offspring of the Sons of God and the daughters of men joining together. They were the Titans of old. Even though many thought they were all destroyed in the Flood, they must not have been because they are still mentioned in various places in the old testament. Case in point, Goliath, and his family among the Philistines.

OUR WEAPONS: FAITH, WEAPON OF POWER

> *For though we walk in the flesh, we do not war according to the flesh. For the weapons of our warfare are not carnal but mighty in God for pulling down strongholds, casting down arguments and every high thing that exalts itself against the knowledge of God, bringing every thought into captivity to the obedience of Christ, and being ready to punish all disobedience when your obedience is fulfilled.* **(2 Corinthians 10:3-6)**

The battle for your soul is raging as you read this chapter and the weapons at your disposal are more powerful than any weapon ever to be conceived by the mind of humanity. This is a very broad statement, but there is no other way to say it. Every weapon used in the name of the Lord Jesus Christ will level strongholds. The key to understanding the power of these weapons of God is in the level of faith in your life. Your faith in the Lord corresponds to power of God in your life. Just because you pray in other tongues or the loudest in the room does not make your prayers more powerful. This does not make you more righteous in the eyes of the Lord. The Apostle Paul says that the weapons of our warfare are of the spiritual nature and not carnal. They are mighty in God for pulling down strongholds and casting down arguments and every high thing that exalts itself against the knowledge of God. The knowledge of God is truth to which no falsehood can bear.

Jesus spoke against the Pharisees and the religious leaders of the day because of their lack of knowledge, vision, understanding, humility, meekness, and mercy. These are the things that Jesus taught His disciples from the very beginning until His death that it took to be true child of God. Paul also pointed out that we must bring every thought into captivity to the obedience of Christ. Every thought that crosses our minds must be focused on obedience to Christ. If your mind drifts away from the Lord Jesus and what He wants for you, then you need to reevaluate your faith and recalibrate your life. Without faith, you will not be able to withstand the mildest of skirmishes. Refocus your life to have faith in Jesus Christ at the center of your life and everyone who is a part of it.

> ***above all, taking the shield of faith with which you will be able to quench all the fiery darts of the wicked one.*** **(Ephesians 6:16)**

The letter to the Ephesian church is one that focuses much on the notion of unity in the body of believers. This is not just any unity, but it is a unity that is found rooted and grown in faith. Without faith in Christ, then it is just a social club. Unfortunately, many churches in Christianity are glorified social clubs. The Christ-filled congregation is one that exhibits the fruit of faith in every aspect of life, inside and outside the church. If you truly possess the shield of faith as a weapon of warfare in your arsenal, then the adversary will be unable to penetrate your defenses. When the wicked one begins to come against you with his fiery darts, the shield of faith not only stops them from hitting you and causing harm, but it quenches them rendering them powerless. It takes the punch out of Satan's attacks and makes him powerless as well.

In the ancient world and the armies that developed from it, the Spartans, the Assyrians, the Roman Armies all utilized what was known as a shield wall. This was when a group of soldiers, standing shoulder to shoulder and back to back, locked their shields together to form a solid wall of shields. This arrangement was as solid as any wall and was deadly to the enemy. The enemy could not penetrate to you, but you could attack them for a more efficient and effective means of attack in open field combat. The same is with the shield of faith. The more soldiers of the faith lock their shields of faith together, the more effective the attacks and defenses are going to be against the enemy. The shield is one of the few items given both as a weapon and a piece of protective armor.

> ***When the people therefore saw that Jesus was not there, nor His disciples, they also got into boats and came to Capernaum, seeking Jesus. And when they found Him on the other***

> *side of the sea, they said to Him, "Rabbi, when did You come here?"*
>
> *Jesus answered them and said, "Most assuredly, I say to you, you seek Me, not because you saw the signs, but because you ate of the loaves and were filled. Do not labor for the food which perishes, but for the food which endures to everlasting life, which the Son of Man will give you, because God the Father has set His seal on Him."*
>
> *Then they said to Him, "What shall we do, that we may work the works of God?"*
>
> *Jesus answered and said to them, "This is the work of God, that you believe in Him whom He sent."* **(John 6:24-29)**

It is believed that it is a complicated process to do God's will for your life. The difficult part of the sanctified life is in the turning away from your past. The history you lived prior to your conversion to Christ many times will dictate the way you live your Christian life. This is where faith plays a vital role in directing you down the right path. The faith that we show is reflected in our motives and the things of which we are passionate. If you are passionate in the Lord concerning janitorial service to the church, then God will bless the works of your heart. It is not as much what you do as it is where your heart and soul are as you do it. The shield of faith is the crucial piece of weaponry armor used not only to protect the mind, heart, and soul but it used as a weapon to strike the enemy a deadly blow. When you stand firm in the face of the enemy, faith is always your strongest weapon because it always forces the enemy to stand down and in most cases retreat.

The encounter Jesus had with the multitudes was a test of the faith of both the multitudes and the disciples. Jesus saw that their belief was wavering because they lacked understanding. He saw that they followed Him for the food not for belief in Him as the Son of God. He knew that they did not want a sign. This was interesting. It seems that the people here were not wealthy but people who struggled through life every day. This is the reason Jesus had compassion on them. Jesus showed them plainly the truth of the gospel. The presence of Jesus with them was the testimony of the gospel. This is the faith building power of the gospel. Faith is where we build hope in our salvation through the sanctified life to glorification with our Lord. He wanted them to believe in the one who sent Him. Many of those present would say that they believed in God. But, do they believe in the name of God or God the creator and lover of His creation? Do you see God as Father who interacts with His creation or just a God as words on a page? We truly need to stand back and evaluate our faith. You say you believe in Jesus Christ as your Lord and Savior, but do you truly believe that the man Jesus died two thousand years for you or do you just accept it? Do you truly believe this man Jesus was sent by God in heaven, who also is His Father, and that Jesus died and rose from the dead? Many need a sign to be convinced of facts, are you one of those people?

They asked Jesus, **"What shall we do, that we may work the works of God?"** He told them the means of doing the works of God is to believe in the one who sent Him. He did want them to believe superficially as they would normally do. He wanted them to truly believe with all their heart, mind, soul, and strength. Jesus wanted the people to see God the Father in and through the Son. I believe, even today with all the resources at our disposal, that it is harder for the follower or Christian to make a full commitment to the Lord's service in faith. Ask yourself that question as you look to Jesus, the author and finisher of our faith, for guidance in life. What shall we do that we may work the works of God? You must first show your faith relationship with God the Father and then the Son. Most important we must realize the Holy Spirit is just as much part of this faith relationship. What shall we do, you ask? Well, let's start with the searching of the heart and make sure you are allowing the Holy Spirit to guide and lead you in your walk of Faith in Christ. Then the Holy Spirit will help you grow in your faith so that your shield of faith will truly withstand any attack of the enemy.

Therefore they said to Him, "What sign will You perform then, that we may see it and believe You? What work will You do? Our fathers ate the manna in the desert; as it is written, 'He gave them bread from heaven to eat.'"

Then Jesus said to them, "Most assuredly, I say to you, Moses did not give you the bread from heaven, but My Father gives you the true bread from heaven. For the bread of God is He who comes down from heaven and gives life to the world."

Then they said to Him, "Lord, give us this bread always."
(John 6:30-34)

The understanding of the people of Jesus' day was no different than those today. We must see a sign to believe. The average person must see, touch, or smell to believe it to be real. This is not faith! The author of the letter to the Hebrews gives the simplest definition concerning faith; ***Now faith is the substance of things hoped for, the evidence of things not seen.* (Hebrews 11:1)** This is a very simplified definition of faith. The whole of Christian life has its foundation in faith. Apart from faith, there is no hope! Jesus was trying to relay eternal realities with earthly examples. We may see them today, but do we? Do we truly understand what Jesus is telling the people, even His closest disciples, did not understand the analogies? How do expect to understand if you do not seek the Bread that comes from heaven in faith?

So, you are wondering why I went down the road with Jesus as the Bread of heaven. He is the bread of life that came down from heaven to sustain us and keep our hope alive. Also, it is this faith that is the true representation of the shield of faith as a spiritual weapon given by God. It is in this faith, this shield against the enemy, that we will be able to stand strong and be courageous. A solid shield of faith is a strong defense. A solid shield of faith is a strong offense as we pursue God with faith in Jesus Christ through the power of the Holy Spirit. We will defeat the armies of darkness with the light of the world. The people standing before Jesus on that day did not understand this simple concept. Faith is an act of hope and belief uniting together as one.

OUR WEAPONS: AUTHORITY, THE WORD OF GOD

> *And Jesus said to them, "I am the bread of life. He who comes to Me shall never hunger, and he who believes in Me shall never thirst. But I said to you that you have seen Me and yet do not believe. All that the Father gives Me will come to Me, and the one who comes to Me I will by no means cast out. For I have come down from heaven, not to do My own will, but the will of Him who sent Me. This is the will of the Father who sent Me, that of all He has given Me I should lose nothing, but should raise it up at the last day. And this is the will of Him who sent Me, that everyone who sees the Son and believes in Him may have everlasting life; and I will raise him up at the last day."* **(John 6:35-40)**

Faith in Jesus Christ is that which will sustain and empower us for service to Him. The will of the Father rest in the Son. All that was given to the Son will be raised up at the last day. Jesus said that all who see Him and believes in Him will have everlasting life. This is the will of the Father. We may not be able to see Him physically, but when we believe in Him with all our hearts in true faith, then we will see Him and not deny that He is the Son of God. Why do Christians ask this question? Because the enemy pushes doubt and distractions into our routine, both good and bad, to lead our thoughts away from God. We must take our thoughts captive under the power of the Holy Spirit, so we may live the life of faith that God the Father has set before us. Remember what Jesus said to Thomas when he had doubted Jesus had risen from the dead, *"Thomas, because you have seen Me, you have believed. Blessed are those who have not seen and yet have believed"* (John 20:29) Thomas and the other disciples had to see to believe, but we must believe to see.

> *Then Jesus was led up by the Spirit into the wilderness to be tempted by the devil. And when He had fasted forty days and forty nights, afterward He was hungry. Now when the tempter came to Him, he said, "If You are the Son of God, command that these stones become bread."*
>
> *But He answered and said, "It is written, 'Man shall not live by bread alone, but by every word that proceeds from the mouth of God.'"* **(Matthew 4:1-4)**

Jesus, being led by the Holy Spirit, was brought into the wilderness of Judea. This is forests with trees and the underbrush, but it was desolate and desert. After not eating or drinking anything for forty days and nights, you would be at the point of death, if not dead. Jesus, being human, was at His weakest. But Jesus, also being divine, received strength in the human frailties. He found His strength in the words that came from God the Father. The belief that God the Father and Jesus is the word of God personified must be the strength which is the greatest of the weapons in our arsenal. God's glory is evidenced in the person of the Son. Jesus is the Word, who was, who is, and always will be in the lives of those believes and loves Him with all their being. Jesus was the Word who proceeded from the mouth of God. He was speaking of Himself. Do we listen for the words that proceed from the mouth of God? Do Christians realize that if they truly are Christians as Jesus defines for us in the beatitudes of Matthew chapter five, then we will know the Word is all we need in our arsenal of weapons to defeat the enemy.

THE HOLY SPIRIT: GOD'S MIGHT, THE BLACKSMITH AND TRAINER OF GOD'S WEAPONRY

> *And He said to them, "It is not for you to know times or seasons which the Father has put in His own authority. But you shall receive power when the Holy Spirit has come upon you; and you shall be witnesses to Me in Jerusalem, and in all Judea and Samaria, and to the end of the earth."* **(Acts 1:7-8)**

The Battle for Eternity

The Holy Spirit is the one whom the Father has put within us for the purpose of forging His greatest weapon against the forces of the enemy. When Jesus walk the earth, He had the Holy Spirit within Him and was the power of God through Him. No evil could ever come against Him because He was God incarnate, this is true. But He was human as well. He was flesh. And as flesh, the evil adversary thought Him to be vulnerable to attack and therefore defeat. This is the weakness of the enemy. Why is this important? Just as the enemy misunderstood Jesus in His humanity, we must also consider the fact that He will especially misinterpret our walk with Christ as weakness and mistake our humanity and compassion as weakness. Jesus said that in our weakness He is made strongest. In our human weakness and frailty, Christ has made us even stronger than He was, not because we are more God. This is far from the true! We are strongest because He is within us through the same Holy Spirit that resided within Him and comes from the Father. We are forged from the fires of heaven by the molding of the Spirit of God into the image of the Son of God, the Word who became flesh and lived among us and became as we are in life and death. This is how we defeat an eternal foe is with an eternal God who lives with us, in us, and battles through us in all ways. Is God awesome or what?!

5

THE ARMOR OF GOD

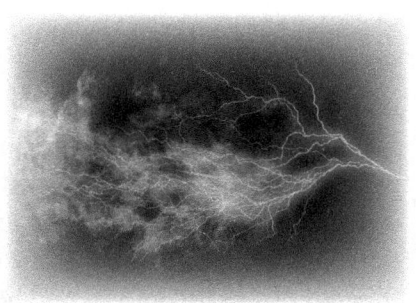

> *Stand therefore, having girded your waist with truth, having put on the breastplate of righteousness, and having shod your feet with the preparation of the gospel of peace; above all, taking the shield of faith with which you will be able to quench all the fiery darts of the wicked one. And take the helmet of salvation, and the sword of the Spirit, which is the word of God; praying always with all prayer and supplication in the Spirit, being watchful to this end with all perseverance and supplication for all the saints—*
> **(Ephesians 6:14-18)**

The full understanding of the gospel of Christ as seen through the eyes of those such as the Apostle Paul and the early church is a true testimony of the faithfulness of the Christ in our lives. Having the armor of God is essential to being able to stand firm in the raging war. The armor, in the time of Paul, was the difference between life and death for a soldier. The roman soldiers were heavily armored the higher the rank they achieved. The higher the rank, the more critical and crucial your status became. When Paul was describing the armor for the Christian, there were key areas that he described as guarded crucial areas of emphasis.

Why do we find this important for Christians? Because, we are in a spiritual battle for our souls. The only way that we can stand strong against the enemy is to be prepared spiritually. Spiritual warfare is the most difficult and demanding of those that fight. Why? Because it is a war that is fought every moment of every day.

The adversary never sleeps, and he never rests or takes the night off. He will find your weakness and exploit it in ways that you cannot imagine. Paul gave us the visual of our protective clothing when going into battle with the evil one. We are all ministers of the gospel of Jesus Christ and are called to the front line in the battle for eternity. Remember, if you die in this war defending the faith and our Lord and Savior Jesus Christ, then you will receive the white robes of His righteousness and be called up in the clouds when He calls His people home.

WAIST GIRDED WITH TRUTH

> *These are the things you shall do: Speak each man the truth to his neighbor; Give judgment in your gates for truth, justice, and peace;* **(Zechariah 8:16)**

Truth of the gospel must encompass the core of your being for you to be protected from the evil one to the center of your being. This was referring to the belt that is wrapped securely around the waist. The belt supports the core of the body during battle. Also, it is one of the first items to be put on of the armor. The belt gathers the tunic together that covers the body of the soldier. The tunic is cinched close by the belt so that it does not hamper movement or the drawing of any weapons. The belt is the brings a sense of security and confidence to the soldier in battle. It is where some of the key weapons that are crucial to our survival are carried. This belt also supports the soldier in battle when they carried much weight for long distances.

The truth of the gospel of Jesus Christ is the same in that it is the truth that must rest at the core of our being. The Christian life, if it is led truly as Jesus has commanded, is demanding and apart from the truth of the gospel, is a difficult way of life. But, through the power of the Holy Spirit, we will walk in power and authority despite the storms and persecution. The belt girded around the waist of the soldier gives the needed support and security to empower them for extended battles. Truth should be found at the core of our being. God knows your heart and knows when the truth, His Truth, is twisted or watered down to tickle the ears of those with deep pockets. The Truth of the Gospel of Jesus Christ is the righteousness of God and nothing is purer as to its intent. The prophet Zechariah prophesies to the things that we should not do with His Truth.

> *Let none of you think evil in your heart against your neighbor; And do not love a false oath. For all these are things that I hate,' Says the LORD.* **(Zechariah 8:17)**

He says not to even think evil in your hearts toward your neighbor. Who is my neighbor? When Jesus said to love your neighbor as you love yourself, what do you think He meant? The obvious answer is "the person who lives next door to me or on my street." Jesus always took the rule or law to the next level. Remember that Jesus said that He came not to abolish the law but to fulfill it. You must have nothing but goodness in your heart and never speak evil against anyone. But, you speak to one another in truth according to the Spirit of Christ in your life. God's righteous Truth is one core element that can be manipulated but must stay true in love. If you truly love the Lord Jesus Christ with all your heart mind soul and strength, then at the core of your being is firmly girded by the Truth of Christ in your life.

> *But you have not so learned Christ, if indeed you have heard Him and have been taught by Him, as the truth is in Jesus: that you put off, concerning your former conduct, the old man which grows corrupt according to the deceitful lusts, and be renewed in the spirit of your mind, and that you put on the new man which was created according to God, in true righteousness and holiness.* **(Ephesians 4:20-24)**

The Truth is found in Jesus and we must live as He lives in our lives. We are new creations when we come into a relationship with Jesus Christ and receive Him as our Lord and Savior. ***Jesus said to him, "I am the way, the truth, and the life. No one comes to the Father except through Me.*** **(John 14:6)** Jesus is the One who gives us His truth to gird ourselves for service to a Holy God. The Apostle Paul was encouraging the church in Ephesus to move forward in their faith and know that Jesus is truly the Lord of their lives. He said that they must put away anything that is contrary to the teachings of Christ. Because they are now a new man in Christ and the truth of the Gospel of Jesus Christ is in them. So, they must live the life that the Spirit of God has led them to live. You are a new creation being renewed in the spirit of your mind. In this, you will live in the true righteousness and holiness of God. Truth is only found solely in One man who is the Son of God. The Truth that you gird about your waist is that of the Son of God.

> *And the Word became flesh and dwelt among us, and we beheld His glory, the glory as of the only begotten of the Father, full of grace and truth.*
> *John bore witness of Him and cried out, saying, "This was He of whom I said, 'He who comes after me is preferred before me, for He was before me.'"*
> *And of His fullness we have all received, and grace for grace. For the law was given through Moses, but grace and truth came through Jesus Christ.* **(John 1:14-17)**

The grace and truth of God was given to us through Jesus the Christ, His Son. Even John, the beloved disciple of Jesus, saw the importance of not only knowing Jesus, but acknowledging and living His truth in everything we say and do. The truth of Christ must reside within the core of our existence and therefore we live our lives for Him. So, it is of the most importance that we gird ourselves in the Truth of Christ to be protected and called of the Living God.

The Breastplate of Righteousness

> *Stand therefore, having girded your waist with truth, having put on the breastplate of righteousness,* **(Ephesians 6:14)**

The breastplate is a crucial part of the armor because it is essential for the protection of the heart. The heart, for the Christian, is the place where the Spirit of God or the Holy Spirit exists. Because the heart of the individual can be penetrated from all sides, the breastplate is in place to protect the one who wears it from harm on all sides. Because you have girded yourself with the Truth of the Gospel of Christ, then, the protection of your heart and soul comes next with the Breastplate of Righteousness. The breastplate becomes stronger and more enduring as one grows in their faith. Every part of the armor of God has one purpose. The purpose of the armor is to protect the wearer from the attacks of the enemy. If there are weaknesses or cracks in the armor, the enemy will exploit and be able to destroy the wearer of the armor. The beauty of its strength and coverage is that it covers front and back. The enemy does not always attack from the front. Even though we look for the strongest attacks from the front, our enemy, Satan, attacks your area of most vulnerability.

> *"You shall make the breastplate of judgment. Artistically woven according to the workmanship of the ephod you shall make it: of gold, blue, purple, and scarlet thread, and fine woven linen, you shall make it."* (Exodus 28:15)

God specifically designed the priestly garments. Each part of the vestment was placed for a purpose in the rituals of the High Priest, Aaron being the first. Every stone and design of each woven part of the breastplate had a purpose. Many times, God is truly unusually precise in the design of something to be certain the commitment and obedience of the person to whom He is directing the design. In this part of Exodus, the design of all garments of the priests including Aaron, Moses brother, set in motion the ritual ceremonies that are characteristic of the ones who worship the God of Heaven. The first of the monotheistic religions of the ancient world. The parts of the breastplate had representations that reflected the Israelite state and its connection to the glory of God. For example, there were four rows of three various precious stones inlayed within the breastplate. Each stone represented each of the twelve tribes of Israel. The High priest would wear this as he entered the Holy Place. He was representing the twelve tribes of Israel to God. The colors of the thread were another specific part of the making of the garment. As with the making of the Ephod, the colors were specific and had meaning to the Lord God. Gold, blue, purple and scarlet thread were used woven in a squared pattern.

Another interesting aspect of the breastplate of the priest was the fact that it was called the "breastplate of judgement." We look at the parts of the priestly garments as those items that are representative of essential glory to God. But, this item of the garment is representative of the protection from the divine judgement of God. It is a piece of priestly armor. The question is how it will protect you from the judgement, providing the priest's heart is right with God, otherwise he is struck down and killed by God.

> *But now the righteousness of God apart from the law is revealed, being witnessed by the Law and the Prophets, even the righteousness of God, through faith in Jesus Christ, to all and on all who believe. For there is no difference; for all have sinned and fall short of the glory of God, being justified freely by His grace through the redemption that is in Christ Jesus, whom God set forth as a propitiation by His blood, through faith, to demonstrate His righteousness, because in His forbearance God had passed over the sins that were previously committed, to demonstrate at the present time His righteousness, that He might be just and the justifier of the one who has faith in Jesus.* **(Romans 3:21-26)**

The righteousness of God is the solid foundation for our strength as believers. The breastplate of righteousness, therefore, serves as the protection for our heart and soul. The righteousness of God is given to all those who believe in His Son and that He sent the Son. He shows no partiality because God's righteousness has more to do with faith than works. Paul is has given a lengthy discourse in his letter to the believers in Rome where he defends the righteousness of God as the golden thread woven through the fabric of salvation. When our heart and soul is protected by the righteousness of God, then we find peace, strength, and security in our walk with Him. Remember that you are no better than the sinner that you are speaking with because all have sinned and fallen short of the glory of God. Through the righteousness of His grace, we find redemption that is in Christ Jesus. All who look to Jesus and believe in Him as Lord and Savior are justified by faith.

Righteousness is defined as the state of being, acting per divine or moral law, and being free from guilt or sin. This is defined by the Merriam-Webster dictionary. The act of righteousness and the righteousness that resides with God and the individual is the same, when it acts within the perimeters of divine and moral laws. As Christians understand righteousness, it resides on the moral compass of truth and purity of heart that sets the person on the right path and holds them there as they live their lives for God through Jesus Christ. If we live free from guilt or sin, we live in the righteousness of God. The breastplate of righteousness protects the Christian, who puts it on, from attacks of the heart and soul that the enemy delivers.

SHOD THE FEET TO SPREAD THE GOSPEL OF PEACE

> ***and having shod your feet with the preparation of the gospel of peace;*** **(Ephesians 6:15)**

For most people, your feet are important to your survival in the everyday world. But, for the Christian, the feet are important because it is what moves them forward and outward to carry the gospel of Jesus Christ to those who need to hear it. When Paul speaks of the feet in this verse, he refers to the protection of Christ in the Holy Spirit. What does that mean? It means that the gospel cannot be spread and delivered without moving forward. The feet, whether physically or spiritually, are means by which the movement takes place. Christ covers us with the anointing of the Holy Spirit to carry the gospel of peace to those who must hear it and be saved. The feet support you in the delivery and the covering of the feet provides protection, peace, and therefore a means of strength as you follow the call of God for His glory. When the Christian steps out in faith to carry the gospel of Christ into the world, their way is prepared for the task. The feet are representative of the stepping out in faith with power, confidence, and authority to deliver the message of eternal life to the lost.

> *"These things I have spoken to you while being present with you. But the Helper, the Holy Spirit, whom the Father will send in My name, He will teach you all things, and bring to your remembrance all things that I said to you. Peace I leave with you, My peace I give to you; not as the world gives do I give to you. Let not your heart be troubled, neither let it be afraid."* **(John 14:25-27)**

Jesus encouraged the disciples on many occasions concerning His death. Their fear and uncertainty caused them on more than one occasion to falter in their faith of Him. This is truly when uncertainty and fear filter into your life. The disciples had experienced every aspect of Jesus' life and ministry, so their confusion was warranted considering the news that they were given. When you are given the peace of the good news or the gospel, it is real and tangible as well as powerful for stepping out in faith. Jesus wanted them to be readied in their spirits for the trials to come. The Holy Spirit was the prophesied comforter, helper, teacher, and the one who brings peace to your soul. Peace comes in the life of the believer when there is no waiver from the faith. Peace comes when a believer accepts what the Holy Spirit, the Spirit of God, reveals in your life. Jesus comforted His disciples with the peace that surrounded Him. This peace is from the Holy Spirit that resides within Him. No one could put their figure on what made Jesus stand out from the other Rabbis and teachers, even the prophets of the day. But it was the peace of God that passes all understanding and comprehension that attracted multitudes to Him.

Jesus told His disciples that it was the same peace of God that He possessed was the peace that He was leaving them. This peace, like everything else given by God, was to be given away to others. I believe that it was a little while before they understood this completely. Jesus also encouraged the disciples by telling them this peace was purely separate from the peace of the world. The "Pax Romano," which was the peace of Rome, was only peace if you followed the harsh and even sometimes deadly rule of the Roman Empire. The peace of the world was rooted in this form of peace. It was only enjoyed and profited by those of the aristocrats who were faithful to Rome. The lower and middle class of people of the empire only enjoyed this peace if they laid low and out of the center of attention. The peace of Christ is the opposite of the world.

> *"Now whatever city or town you enter, inquire who in it is worthy, and stay there till you go out. And when you go into a household, greet it. If the household is worthy, let your peace come upon it. But if it is not worthy, let your peace return to you."* **(Matthew 10:11-13)**

The peace of Christ is given to those believers who are truly focused on the Will of Christ in faith. When Jesus prepared His disciples to share the gospel with the lost, He focused on the lost people of Israel. As a part of tradition, when you enter a person's home, you bring the peace to the home if they welcome you in. In these verses, Jesus is instructing His disciples on the proper way in enter a home. But, it is not just about entering the home, though this is a crucial part of proper form. The important lesson they were to learn here was concerning the power and authority that they possess. The peace of God is only given to those who are going to share it with others. Most Jews would do this as a formality, but to Jesus it means so much more. This is w He tells them that if they find them unworthy of the Blessing of peace, they will take it back and leave. He tells the disciples that it will be far more tolerable for those people of Sodom and Gomorrah than for those who reject the peace and blessing of God. Do we as Christians today reject the true peace and blessings of God and settle on a bad counterfeit version?

The Shield of Faith

> ***Above all, taking the shield of faith with which you will be able to quench all the fiery darts of the wicked one.*** **(Ephesians 6:16)**

The shield is one of the most versatile instruments of warfare at our disposal. In the ancient world, the shield was used both as an offensive and defensive weapon. The most notable use of the shield for the day in warring cultures was the shield wall. The shield wall was a defensive counter measure which was extended by the Romans into the "testudo" or "tortoise" in which shields were locked to prevent attack from the front, sides, back and over-head. Soldiers had the ability as a group by locking their shields into this formation to move into an enemy offensive and breach their defense, so as to destroy the enemies from within.

When we compare the shield of faith in the understanding of today's church with that of the ancient world, we find an obvious progression. But the road was rough and difficult to follow. Many Christians fell along the way because of the lack of faith and unwillingness to endure to the end. Jesus, when He called His disciples, began the task of building their armor to God the Father's specification. Their faith was the piece of armor that was the most carefully molded and formed into God's Will. The way of progression was difficult for the disciples as it is for us today. Therefore, Jesus told them the parable of the sower.

> *Then He spoke many things to them in parables, saying: "Behold, a sower went out to sow. And as he sowed, some seed fell by the wayside; and the birds came and devoured them. Some fell on stony places, where they did not have much earth; and they immediately sprang up because they had no depth of earth. But when the sun was up they were scorched, and because they had no root they withered away. And some fell among thorns, and the thorns sprang up and choked them. But others fell on good ground and yielded a*

crop: some a hundredfold, some sixty, some thirty. He who has ears to hear, let him hear!" **(Matthew 13:3-9)**

The multitudes were not going to understand the parables and their meanings. The disciples looked to Him to teach them the meanings. He explained the parable of the sower to His disciples. He said that anyone who hears the message of the kingdom and does not understand it, then the evil one comes and snatches the word from their hearts. This is the seed that fell along the path. He said that next is the one who hears the word and receives it with joy. But because it was not rooted in faith, it only lasts for a brief time. When the heat of persecution because of the word comes, he then withers, his faith falters and dies. This is the seed that fell on rocky ground. Then, Jesus said there was one who heard the word, but the worries of the world became a distraction and eventually choked out any opportunity for the word to bear any fruit. This is referring to the seed that fell among the thorns. Then, those seeds which fell into good soil were those who hears the word and understands it. These also are able and willing to take the same word and multiply it in the world. The Word of God, who is Jesus Christ our Lord, is our greatest weapon in the eternal war for our souls. The important thing to remember is that the Shield of Faith is used in tandem with the Sword of the Spirit. The Shield is protection for the presentation of the Sword or Word of God. So, keep them both close to your heart and polish and ready for battle. Where are you and your church in this parable of Jesus? Are you ready to take up the Sword of the Spirit which is the Word of God and fight or just fade and wither in the pews of the world?

6

Our Divine Protector

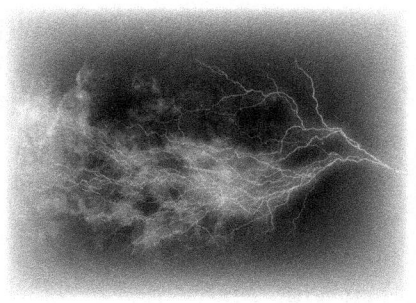

> *And Moses said to the people, "Do not be afraid. Stand still, and see the salvation of the LORD, which He will accomplish for you today. For the Egyptians whom you see today, you shall see again no more forever. The LORD will fight for you, and you shall hold your peace."* **(Exodus 14:13-14)**

Christians today have the belief that they are alone in this war for their souls. This is farther from the truth. God has proven Himself to His creation repeatedly. The beauty of our relationship with our heavenly Father is that He loves us and shows mercy and grace toward us countless times even though we do not deserve it. When Moses spoke to God's people, he knew with conviction that God would provide and protect those who love Him. Why is it so difficult for God's people to have the conviction of faith to truly follow Him? He wants us to love Him. How can you love someone that you never believed in? God the Father loved us so much that He sent His own Son to live and show humanity the way to salvation and eternal rest. He led His people out of the bondage of Egypt to give them salvation and a land of their own.

Moses was telling the Israelites to be still and listen for the Lord and He will speak to you to show you the way to salvation. Humanity, in all their arrogance, always believes more toward the negative rather than the truth. Their sinful nature overtook them, and they reacted out of fear. Their fear came from a lack of control in their lives. If they were to turn away from God and go back to Egypt, then they at least would be aware and somewhat have control over their lives. God, in their minds, was leading them into a situation where they would have to rely on God for everything. Yes! That was the point all along! From the beginning, God has wanted nothing more than for His people, and now all people, to surrender control of everything to Him. The problem was with their faith. Moses tried to tell them to not be afraid and to stand still. The result was to be glorious! He told them that would see the salvation of the Lord. What does that mean?

HE IS THE GOD OF OUR DAILY BATTLES

> ***And the Angel of God, who went before the camp of Israel, moved and went behind them; and the pillar of cloud went from before them and stood behind them. So it came between the camp of the Egyptians and the camp of Israel. Thus it was a cloud and darkness to the one, and it gave light by night to the other, so that the one did not come near the other all that night.* (Exodus 14:19-20)**

The Divine protection given to the people of Israel was provided in their escape from Egypt. God knew the deception of the Pharaoh and the anger that had festered within his heart. God knew that Pharaoh had no other choice but to pursue the Israelites and return them to Egypt. In God's mighty and most glorious way, He traveled with them as a massive pillar of fire by smoke by day and a pillar of fire by night. But, the relentlessness of the Egyptian army and Pharaoh overwhelmed the efforts of the Israelites in their exodus. When the Israelites were backed up to the sea with the Egyptian armies in readiness for pursuit, God stepped in and told Moses to stand and hold the staff high and deliverance will be provided. As Moses lift the staff high above his head, the waters of the sea parted, and the Israelites walked across on dry ground.

The armies of Pharaoh searched for way to surpass the Pillar of protection of the Lord God, but there was none. God even made the wheels of their chariots fall off to stay their pursuit. Once the Israelites were safely to the other side of the sea, God released the armies to continue pursuit. But when they all finally entered the sea, God returned the sea to its normal state and the waters crashed down upon the armies of Pharaoh and they all were drowned in the sea.

Today's religious society has no concept of the power of God and that He truly takes a special interest in our protection. The stories of the Bible are not just stories, but they are real life experiences given to us as learning tools. God wanted us today to learn from the mistakes of others. This was an act of faith and obedience for the Israelites and Moses. Did they walk through the sea by faith or fear? Do not know, but they stepped out trusting God to protect them and He did.

> ***Behold, I send an Angel before you to keep you in the way and to bring you into the place which I have prepared. Beware of Him and obey His voice; do not provoke Him, for He will not pardon your transgressions; for My name is in Him. But if you indeed obey His voice and do all that I speak, then I will be an enemy to your enemies and an adversary to your adversaries.* (Exodus 23:20-22)**

The Lord God has always been the champion for His people. We should in the fact know that God is our protector. Do not rest in the glory of man but the righteousness of God. God is sending His angel as a protector for His people. Remember, even when you think that your back is against the wall, God will give you an escape and a means to defeat His enemies. God told them that His name is in him. This means that when the angel speaks, they follow the instruction because the angel only speaks and does the commands of God. God is our protector through means that we are not aware of as we go through our daily lives. He said that if they would obey the voice of the angel, then your enemies will be His enemies and your adversaries will be His adversaries. As a Christian, who is struggling to lead a Godly life in Christ, we should note that when God is your protector then we will be victorious. Amen!

> *"Be strong and courageous; do not be afraid nor dismayed before the king of Assyria, nor before all the multitude that is with him; for there are more with us than with him. With him is an arm of flesh; but with us is the LORD our God, to help us and to fight our battles." And the people were strengthened by the words of Hezekiah king of Judah.*
> **(2 Chronicles 32:7-8)**

Hezekiah, as king of Judah, was standing against a mighty adversary in king Sennacherib of Assyria. Sennacherib had sent word out blaspheming the Lord God and attempting to turn the people and the armies of Judah and their allies against Hezekiah. Hezekiah knew the Lord God would care for and protect them. The Assyrian army under king Sennacherib was the largest and mightiest in the known world of the day. Hand to hand in combat, the armies of Judah were no match for the destructive force of the Assyrian army. But Hezekiah knew that God would defeat any army, no matter how great and mighty. He believed and stood strong in the fact that God will protect His people, if they would obey His words. The glory of God can only be seen through the faith of the one who sets the example of faith to others. The armies of Assyria were mighty, and king Sennacherib was among the most ruthless when it came to conquest and acquiring nations to further his empire. But God proved Himself to be ruler of all things and nothing Sennacherib had as his means of destruction could even measure the power of one Angel of the Lord. As God told them would happen, it happened.

The armies of Sennacherib were destroyed by the armies of Judah as directed by the Angel of the Lord. King Sennacherib fled to his palace where he was murdered by two of his sons. God is the protector of the weak.

> *Then David said to Saul, "Let no man's heart fail because of him; your servant will go and fight with this Philistine."*

And Saul said to David, "You are not able to go against this Philistine to fight with him; for you are a youth, and he a man of war from his youth."

But David said to Saul, "Your servant used to keep his father's sheep, and when a lion or a bear came and took a lamb out of the flock, I went out after it and struck it, and delivered the lamb from its mouth; and when it arose against me, I caught it by its beard, and struck and killed it. Your servant has killed both lion and bear; and this uncircumcised Philistine will be like one of them, seeing he has defied the armies of the living God." Moreover David said, "The LORD, who delivered me from the paw of the lion and from the paw of the bear, He will deliver me from the hand of this Philistine." **(1 Samuel 17:32-37)**

The stories of the constant battles between Israel and the Philistines remained one of the longest on-going bitter warring of Israel's history. David, a young boy at the time, spent his time with the Lord God and tending his father's sheep. While his brothers were developing their physical fighting skills in preparation for battle, David was preparing himself for the spiritual battles that are about to take place. The soldiers of Israel feared the Philistines because of the giants that fought with them. Goliath was one such giant. Goliath went out every day for six weeks taunting the army of Israel to provoke them to fight. The Israelite army, king Saul and David's brothers included, coward in fear out of intimidation because of Goliath's massive size and apparent strength.

David made his case before the king that he had defeated both a lion and a bear in defense of a lamb. This young man is no different than you and me. Saul did not take him seriously. His faith was demonstrated in his statement *"The LORD, who delivered me from the paw of the lion and from the paw of the bear, He will deliver me from the hand of this Philistine"* (1 Samuel 17:37). If only we, as Christians today, could exhibit such faith. God as our protector will always fight for us and with us in all our battles of life, but we need the faith to allow Him. When David stood against the boastful giant Goliath, he did not stand in defense of himself, the king, not even the nation of Israel. David stood strong in the power of his faith in God and because Goliath was blaspheming the God of Israel, his God. David had a personal relationship with the Lord God that none of the others had, not even his brothers, and it was evident in his actions and was exhibited in his faith. David was successful in defeating the giant Goliath not because of his skill with the sling and stone, but because he trusted and loved the Lord God Almighty. Do we have faith in God for everything as David? Or, do we choose to turn and run from the chance to display the power of God before men and to glorify Him in all things?

GOD IS OUR DEFENSE IN TIMES OF DISTRESS

> *But let all those rejoice who put their trust in You;*
> *Let them ever shout for joy, because You defend them;*
> *Let those also who love Your name*
> *Be joyful in You.*
> *For You, O LORD, will bless the righteous;*
> *With favor You will surround him as with a shield.*
> **(Psalm 5:11-12)**

The Lord God is always there to protect His people and stand at their defense. The glory of the Lord is evidenced in His defense of His people. The big picture begs the question, are you trusting God the Father and the Son to be your defender in your faith? Trust in the Lord is the beginning of knowledge and understanding in the growth to maturity in the faith. Believing is only the start. As you grow in the Lord toward sanctification and the sanctified life, you must note that the only way to maturity in the faith is through the belief that He is there with us and defends us against the enemy. We cannot do it on our own. When an individual put on the armor of God (Ephesians 6:10-20), they have the full protection and defense of God at their disposal. Why, then, if this the case, are Christians so reluctant to trust God and allow Him to defend the ones that He loves? You would defend those who you love, wouldn't you?

The Lord God will not only defend and protect those who love and worship Him, but He will surround them with host on all sides. When God blesses, He guards and protects your front as you move forward spreading the gospel, as He commanded. Jesus, also, defends and protects you at your back and sides. Why is this important? The enemy never comes at you straight at your front, so you see him coming. The enemy attacks from ways that you will never expect to make you fall easier. Be on your guard and know that there is One who always watches your back. Trust and know in the Lord Jesus Christ and have faith in Him.

> *In You, O Lord, I put my trust;*
> *Let me never be ashamed;*
> *Deliver me in Your righteousness.*
> *Bow down Your ear to me,*
> *Deliver me speedily;*
> *Be my rock of refuge,*
> *A fortress of defense to save me.*
> **(Psalm 31:1-2)**

The Lord Jesus is mighty in all His defenses. Remember that He is your mediator with the Father in heaven. Put your trust in Him and always have faith. One must truly stand firm in the belief that we need not be ashamed of the gospel of Jesus Christ. If we are ashamed of Him in the world, then He will be ashamed of you before the Father in heaven. In Psalm 31, David is being sought out to be killed by King Saul. David was being pursued by Saul's elite armies, but with God's help, he eluded his pursuers. David had total trust in the Lord God as his protector and refuge. Why is this so difficult for His people today? The church professes Jesus Christ as Savior, but there is a true lack of belief in Him as Lord. Why? Do we not teach or even preach to God's people today that He is a God of refuge and strength?

What do you think of when you think of a fortress? A castle or city with thick walls surrounding it as a defense, right? What type of fortress do you believe God can build? He is our fortress. What an amazing Truth! If you believe this, then you are well on your way to having the creator of all as your protector. David believed this truth with all his heart and he lived it out from his childhood even until his death. You may not believe that God protects you when you are going through the storms of life. The storms of life are what makes us look to Him because our weaknesses are manifested in us. In many cases, they are even revealed to others. We must be transparent before God and man to be considered blameless. True, we are all sinners saved by grace, but, with that same understanding, we need the protector with us as we struggle through the storm. The important lesson to learn from the storms of life is to trust the Lord Jesus and know that He is with you. When this is learned, then you will be able to stand firm on the rock and in the refuge of His fortress as David did as he ran from Saul and his armies.

> *For thus the L*ORD *has spoken to me:*
> *"As a lion roars,*
> *And a young lion over his prey*
> *(When a multitude of shepherds is summoned against him,*
> *He will not be afraid of their voice*
> *Nor be disturbed by their noise),*
> *So the L*ORD *of hosts will come down*
> *To fight for Mount Zion and for its hill.*
> *Like birds flying about,*
> *So will the L*ORD *of hosts defend Jerusalem.*
> *Defending, He will also deliver it;*
> *Passing over, He will preserve it."*
> **(Isaiah 31:4-5)**

The people of Israel had wavering faith in the Lord God and His protection. They had moments of failings in their faith, but in His heart and faithfulness to His chosen people He was true to His promises. God is always the divine protector to those who are faithful to Him and live according to His commandments and Word. This passage in Isaiah 31 speaks to the understanding that God is always present with us. This passage does speak of the nation of Israel, but this is also true for the church today. Jesus is our advocate to the Father. Because we love and serve the Son in the

Spirit, we have access to the Heavenly Hosts. What a reward! The divine protection we seek is not difficult to see, all we must do is stop the distractions of life, look to Him, and listen with all our heart. He will hear our cry and will answer our plea.

The glory of the Lord God is shown through His Son. The sacrifice that He made for all humanity is the cornerstone of the His divine protection. This is the beauty of the faith that we share in Christ. It is by His stripes that we are healed. For the people of God to become the true people of God, we must first believe that He is who He says He is and accept that as truth. Second, we must desire the things of His righteousness and seek His face. Lastly, we must follow Him with all our heart, mind, soul, and strength. When we do these things, then we will trust Him to live in worship, love, and praise to His glory every moment of every day. Are you ready to truly trust Him with everything and everyone in your life? Are you ready to take up the standard of Christ in the power of the Holy Spirit against the enemies in the spiritual realms both great and small?

7
OUR DIVINE PROTECTION

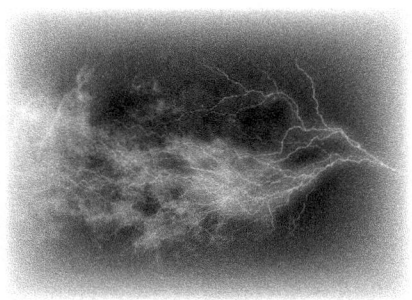

> *So he answered, "Do not fear, for those who are with us are more than those who are with them." And Elisha prayed, and said, "LORD, I pray, open his eyes that he may see." Then the LORD opened the eyes of the young man, and he saw. And behold, the mountain was full of horses and chariots of fire all around Elisha.* **(2 Kings 6:16-17)**

The divine protection that God gives those who love Him is overwhelming for humanity to understand. This is because the human mind and ability to grasp the divine is limited in its capacity understand the divine. God's ways are not our ways and our ways are not God's ways and so we tend to complicate and over analyze those things that are done simply. The divine protection is not just something that is called down from the heavens by a truly faithful servant of God. The divine protection is always given by God and given in abundance for the preservation of those who love Him and live by His commandments.

The wonderful miracles of God are manifested in the faith of those who love Him and follow Him. While Elisha followed and learned from Elijah the marvelous works of God, his only request was that he would obtain double the blessing of Elijah. He asked Elijah for his mantle. This not only meant his cloak, but everything that came with having the power of God only a call away. The aspect of this that concerned Elijah was if Elisha was fully committed to God in his heart. The power of God is not to be taken lightly and we must be continually in prayer with Him. In this story in the life of Elisha, his servant was overwhelmed with fear because the Syrian armies had come down to surround the city. Elisha prayed a simple prayer of faith to the Lord to reveal and confirm to his servant that the heavenly hosts were surrounding the Syrians. In the mountains were chariots of fire prepared to defend Elisha and his armies against Syrians.

We should be encouraged by this time where we see that God's hand is never shortened when it concerns those who love Him. The servant saw the full scope of God's mighty hands at work. The next act of mercy by both Elisha and God shows that He always makes a way that departs from the wrath they deserve. On this occasion, instead of Elisha calling for the release of death and destruction, he prayed another simple prayer that He would only blind them. God blind the entire Syrian army and led the army into the hands of the Israelite king. He led them to the downtown area of Samaria, the capital city of the northern kingdom of Israel. Not understanding what was going on, the king asked if he should have them all killed. Elisha, knowing God's will in the situation, told the king not kill them but feed them and give them drink. In obedience to the prophet, the king fed and gave drink to the blind Syrian army. Then, Elisha prayed another prayer for the army to receive their sight and they did receive their sight. Elisha did something that even shocked the king. He told the king to send them back to their king. This was the will of God. How is our faith in times of trials? Do we believe in faith in our hearts as Elisha did or do we cower in fear at the sight of our enemies? We are protected from the enemy by God in His Word and by His Word. God sent His armies to protect Elisha and his encampment because of his faith. Do you believe this with all your heart?

Divine Protection: Comes from the Lord

Those who trust in the Lord
Are like Mount Zion,
Which cannot be moved, but abides forever.

> *As the mountains surround Jerusalem,*
> *So the* LORD *surrounds His people*
> *From this time forth and forever.*
> **(Psalm 125:1-2)**

The divine protection is for those who love and fear the Lord God with all their heart. The protection is not just for the moment, but it is forever. This should bring strength in that you do not have to worry whether the Lord God has your back. He has your back forever. The beauty of this is the picture that the psalmist paints for the reader. He said that those who trust in the Lord are like Mount Zion that cannot be moved but abides forever. This is incredible because of what this tells us about the relationship between the Lord and His people. Those people have faith that they stand strong in the toughest of times. The Lord is the strength of those who trust in Him forever.

The next verse tells the story that should cause the believer to take notice. He says that as the mountains surround Jerusalem, the Lord also surrounds His people. He does not just surround us as on a plain and flat area. The Lord surrounds those who truly trust Him as the mountains. High above and even below them, where they are at that moment. But, wonderful and merciful beauties of the Lord's love is understood in the fact that His divine protection does surround us forever, even when we do not know it.

DIVINE PROTECTION: GOD HONORS OUR REQUESTS FROM THE HEART

> *So when the Syrians came down to him, Elisha prayed to the* LORD, *and said, "Strike this people, I pray, with blindness." And He struck them with blindness according to the word of Elisha.* **(2 Kings 6:18)**

The Syrians were a true thorn in the flesh of the Israelites of the northern kingdom. Despite the truces and peaceable times, there were also reasons to war against Israel. The basic reason was for the sole purpose of land conquest. This army, led by Ben-Hadad king of Syria, was indecisive at best. The servant of Elisha saw that their backs were against the wall as they were surrounded. But the Elisha knew the plan of God was true and the divine protection will not be defeated. Elisha show his servant and us as the reader that there is always a choice. God's plan is never one-sided. There is always a "safe way" and a "better way." These are the choices that we are given to make regarding our own lives. Elisha could have called the armies of God that were in place and ready for war to destroy the Syrian armies, but he made the better choice. He chose to spare their lives. So, he prayed to the Lord God to strike them with blindness.

God intervened in the lives of His people on many occasions but never at the expense of the free will that He gave them to exercise. They also had a choice. There was choice as a third option to do according to their own decision and do nothing. How do we as a church exercise our free will? Do we ask for God's assistance only to follow our own way? Or, do we truly seek the best option that God gives us? There is a lot to consider as we make decisions in our lives and in our churches today. All that Elisha faced were insurmountable odds. Many would lay down arms and accept defeat in surrender, but not Elisha. He knew God was in control and he had faith that God trusted him to make the best decision for God's people.

> **For the Lord had caused the army of the Syrians to hear the noise of chariots and the noise of horses—the noise of a great army; so they said to one another, "Look, the king of Israel has hired against us the kings of the Hittites and the kings of the Egyptians to attack us!" Therefore they arose and fled at twilight, and left the camp intact—their tents, their horses, and their donkeys—and they fled for their lives. (2 Kings 7:6-7)**

In this moment, God had reacted on His own accord when the Syrians returned for an attempt on the city of Samaria. Elisha was unaware of the circumstances, but the divine protection came. The heavenly host may not have attacked, but as honoring

The Battle for Eternity

the previous actions of the man of God Elisha He caused them to flee. The sounds were as the many armies of the Egyptians and the Hittites. The sounds of many horses and chariots all around them. The Syrian armies were already spooked because of the last encounter with the God of Elisha. They fled so quickly that they left everything behind including all their belongings, donkeys, horses, dwellings, and food. As the small group from went to the camp to verify the report, they also saw that the army shed their garments and weapons as they fled back to Syria. This was confirmation that was reported to the king that the report was true. The people then went unto the camp and gathered the food and scavenged everything left behind by the Syrian army. Then the famine was relieved by the Lord. The work of God to be noted is that He does not always choose to destroy the enemy and He is faithful to those who are faithful and love Him as Elisha had been.

Divine Protection: God sends personal assistance

> *Now when Daniel knew that the writing was signed, he went home. And in his upper room, with his windows open toward Jerusalem, he knelt down on his knees three times that day, and prayed and gave thanks before his God, as was his custom since early days.* **(Daniel 6:10)**

Daniel's prayer was truly faithful to God in all things. There is much that we can learn from the prayer life of Daniel. He was there in Babylon under several kings during the captivity of Jerusalem and the kingdom of Judah. The seventy years that God allowed them to be captive to the Babylonians was long and gave the people of God time to sort through the issues that had accumulated over the years of evil rule and leadership that had led them from God. Prophets like Daniel, Ezekiel and others held the nations together and became their strength and connection with God.

Though Daniel was regarded highly by the king, there were hard and true laws that even the king had to uphold. Worshipping the king was one of those laws that were followed even by the surrounding Medes and Persians. Once the king of the kingdom signed the decree into law, it could not be changed. Darius did not know or even consider the effect that this decree would have on Daniel or any of his servants when he made to sign it. Those closest to him did not tell him the consequences. Darius respected Daniel and his God. His hands were tied because once he made a decree and signed it, it was law and could not be changed. This decree was made so Daniel would be killed and removed from the picture. Those advisers to the king saw Daniel as a threat to them and their position in relation to the king. Daniel had risen to prominence in the kingdom and was positioned next to the king. Jealousy and envy are usually the occasion for deception and attacks toward people of God. This is the reason for the attacks on Daniel. So, king Darius had no choice but to follow his own decree and law. Daniel was thrown in the lion's den as punishment for not worshipping king Darius but worshipping his own God. What would you have done if you were Daniel? What will you do when faced with a decision like Daniel? Will you fold under the pressure and follow the ways of the world or will you follow God?

DIVINE PROTECTION: THE DECEPTION OF THE ADVERSARY

> *Then these men assembled and found Daniel praying and making supplication before his God. And they went before the king, and spoke concerning the king's decree: "Have you not signed a decree that every man who petitions any god or man within thirty days, except you, O king, shall be cast into the den of lions?"* **(Daniel 6:11-12)**

The prayer life of Daniel was well known and the men trying snare Daniel paid attention to the times. They picked a time in which to go to the king and report. The time of Daniel's prayer was perfect because it was proof in their eyes of the deception and rejection of the king and his laws by Daniel. They specifically went to the king and reminded him of the decree to force his hand to honor it no matter the consequences. The idea was not only to kill Daniel but that the blood would be on the hands of the king. Darius could not go against his own law.

> ***Let every soul be subject to the governing authorities. For there is no authority except from God, and the authorities that exist are appointed by God.* (Romans 13:1)**

> ***For he is God's minister to you for good. But if you do evil, be afraid; for he does not bear the sword in vain; for he is God's minister, an avenger to execute wrath on him who practices evil. Therefore you must be subject, not only because of wrath but also for conscience' sake.* (Romans 13:4-5)**

Knowing what we know of the writings of Paul in the letter to the Romans, how would we follow this decree? Paul tells the Roman church to submit to the authorities. Daniel draw the line when it came to worship of the king. During the time of the Apostle Paul, the Emperor of the Roman Empire thought of himself as god-emperor. This was like the Pharaohs in Egypt of ancient times. You see where that got them. So, Daniel felt the same way when he was told to worship the king as god and bow down to him. Those leaders who were deceiving the king against Daniel had formulated a plan that could not fail. Because even as the Apostle Paul had wrote those words down in the letter to the Romans, there was great persecution that he would himself partake and die at the cruel hand of the emperor Nero. The point is in relation to what we speak of here is that God has pointed the leaders and kings to govern for the good. If they go the path of evil, then they will to God for that reign. Our part is to submit and let God reign. Is Jesus the love of your life and are you willing to trust the divine protection provided by the One who has saved your soul? Are we as a people of God and heirs to the promises of God through His Son Jesus Christ, willing to do what it takes walk in the power of the hand and protection of Almighty God?

Divine Protection: Sent by God

Now the king went to his palace and spent the night fasting; and no musicians were brought before him. Also his sleep went from him. Then the king arose very early in the morning and went in haste to the den of lions. And when he came to the den, he cried out with a lamenting voice to Daniel. The king spoke, saying to Daniel, "Daniel, servant of the living God, has your God, whom you serve continually, been able to deliver you from the lions?" **(Daniel 6:18-20)**

The protection of God was not just from the angel of God sent to Daniel in the den. The protection was sent to the king. The king was exceeding troubled about the events concerning Daniel. He was not concerned whether Daniel worshiped him. Darius knew his commitment to his God and Darius feared his God. If Daniel was praying to his God, Darius knew that this set him apart as an exception that he was unable accommodate. Darius ran to the pit that Daniel was thrown into and he lamented over it. This means that he wailed and cried over it. But God was in control of the whole situation. I believe that when Darius asked the question as he called out, he knew the answer in the back of his mind, or he would not have gone to the pit himself. He would have sent someone to check it out.

8

The Promises

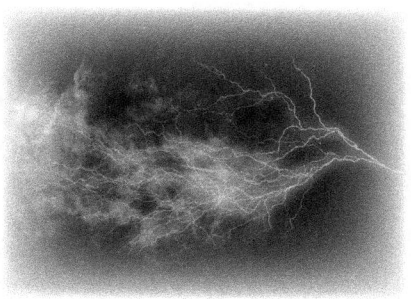

> *For God so loved the world that He gave His only begotten Son, that whoever believes in Him should not perish but have everlasting life. For God did not send His Son into the world to condemn the world, but that the world through Him might be saved.* **(John 3:16-17)**

The promises of God are truly too numerous to count. Regardless to the number of times that we might read or even hear the promises of God through Jesus Christ, we make every effort to make God break them. As hard as we may try make Him break His promises, He will never do it. The promises of God are solid and true. The most popular promise was made by Jesus when He met with Nicodemus in the night. Nicodemus was a Pharisee and one of the Sanhedrin. The common belief is that he was a man who, even though he knew the as his colleagues, he saw something different in Jesus. These two verses in the Gospel of John have resonated in the minds young and old believers alike. This is the single most popular scripture and the most encouraging scripture for Christians. These two verses sum up the totality of God's love for humanity. Looking at the promises of God begins with the Covenants between God and His chosen people and is finally found in the new Covenant with Jesus Christ, His Son, coming to fulfill the promises. In all that we have seen and experienced to this point as the study of spiritual warfare continues, the understanding of how the promises connect down through time and why God wanted to reconcile with a very tainted humanity lay within those two verses. Let us now look at the New Covenant in Jesus Christ, the Son of God. It is in these various passages of scripture that we may find understanding. The "I AM" passages are Jesus' validating His purposes and fulfillment of God's Covenants with His people.

The Promises: I AM!

> *Jesus answered, "If I honor Myself, My honor is nothing. It is My Father who honors Me, of whom you say that He is your God. Yet you have not known Him, but I know Him. And if I say, 'I do not know Him,' I shall be a liar like you; but I do know Him and keep His word. Your father Abraham rejoiced to see My day, and he saw it and was glad."*
>
> *Then the Jews said to Him, "You are not yet fifty years old, and have You seen Abraham?"*
>
> *Jesus said to them, "Most assuredly, I say to you, before Abraham was, I AM."* **(John 8:54-58)**

Jesus decided to simplify the concept for those present. He told them that He is the bread of life. The reason they call these passages the "I AM" scriptures is because in Jesus' revelation of Himself, He uses them to better explain His purpose. In His references to Himself as the I AM, He also makes the reference to the burning bush and Moses' encounter with God (Exodus 3:13-14). Even in this reference, God refers to Himself as I AM, but this is calling back to before Abraham. The beginning of all creation is where God was pointing to for Moses' understanding. The gospel of John, in the beginning of the gospel, gives the reader a clearer insight into Jesus as the great I AM in scripture. No place in scripture better speaks of the role that Jesus as the Son plays in the whole of the creation than in the first verses of the gospel. Why do you think John did it? The gospel of John was written to emphasize the deity of Jesus as the Christ, the Messiah, the Holy Son of God. The I AM passages throughout the gospel truly enhance the discussion because describes Himself in various terms that the disciples, some in the crowds, understand.

THE PROMISES: "I AM THE BREAD OF LIFE" - SPIRITUAL FOOD

> *Then Jesus said to them, "Most assuredly, I say to you, Moses did not give you the bread from heaven, but My Father gives you the true bread from heaven. For the bread of God is He who comes down from heaven and gives life to the world."*
>
> *Then they said to Him, "Lord, give us this bread always."*
>
> *And Jesus said to them, "I am the bread of life. He who comes to Me shall never hunger, and he who believes in Me shall never thirst."* **(John 6:32-35)**

These promises spoken by Jesus are true because He is the Word of God. The people did not understand it because they wanted their stomachs filled. The disciples had a tough time with understanding because they were common everyday people who were seeking a more fulfilled life with God. Jesus said that Moses was not the giver of heavenly bread, God is the only one who can give heavenly bread. So, He said that He is the ***bread of life***. He went on to explain His meaning. Jesus said that the bread of God is He who comes down from heaven. Also, He was saying that this bread or One from heaven will give life to the world. This means that it would not only fill them, but it will fill everyone in the world. They were still not understanding. With the question asked, there was a different level of misunderstanding that only Jesus could see. He saw into the hearts of those who were questioning His statement. If they knew what they were asking and who they were questioning, they would have thought about their response before questioning Him.

The questioning of this puzzling statement brought more clarification by Jesus. He went on to say to them that He is the bread of life. With this statement Jesus clarified even further. He said that whoever comes to Him will not hunger. He referred to the spiritual food. This His disciples would not fully understand until they realized who He really was after the resurrection. The fact that they would not hunger went along with the notion bread being the staple sustenance for life at the time. He appealed them and their knowledge of Jewish history when He referred earlier to the manna that came down from heaven. Jesus not only sustains you for the moment but for life.

Jesus added the idea of thirst in as a part of being fulfilled in Him. He went a step further when He said that whoever believes in Him shall never thirst again. This statement fulfilled the total of the sustenance, not that it was they ate or drank, but it was all needed. God the Father gave us more than enough in Jesus Christ to be sustained throughout eternity. The emphasis with the drink was on the belief of the individual. The offering of bread for life drew them in and their belief sustained them for all eternity. Why? Because the drink that He is referring to is the blood that will shed for all who believe. What an amazing Lord we have! Amen!

> ***On the last day, that great day of the feast, Jesus stood and cried out, saying, "If anyone thirsts, let him come to Me and drink. He who believes in Me, as the Scripture has said, out of his heart will flow rivers of living water." But this He spoke concerning the Spirit, whom those believing in Him would receive; for the Holy Spirit was not yet given, because Jesus was not yet glorified.*** (John 7:37-39)

The last day of the feast of Tabernacles was the most important and therefore all eyes were on Jesus as He stood and cried out. This is important because He wanted everyone including His brothers and the thousands who stood in the courts of the Temple to hear what He had to say. He said that whoever believes in Him will flow from them the Holy Spirit and the love of God. The beauty of this is that this was His first public proclamation as to His identity in connection with God the Father and the Holy Spirit. The people were mixed in their reception of this profession that He would be the One to give them the Holy Spirit. They were confused on the Holy Spirit's identity. The people, the common people, were not being taught concerning the Holy Spirit at this time. There were vague references to the Holy Spirit, but Jesus made constant references to Him, especially concerning Himself. The Holy Spirit was not yet given to everyone else because Jesus had not been glorified.

The rivers of Living Water were references in many portions of Jesus' teachings because it referred to the fact that Jesus was going to send the Holy Spirit after His ascension to His Father. For example, the Samaritan woman (John 4:1-26) at the well referred to the Living Water that He would give those who believe. The belief that Jesus is not only a prophet of God but the Son of God. The Samaritan woman believed and that day she and the entire city came to believe in the Living Water who is Jesus. This is what Jesus was referring to in verse thirty-nine of chapter seven when He spoke of the Living Waters that flowed from the heart. The Holy Spirit would be sent after His ascension. First you must believe in the One who sent Him and then believe in Him.

THE PROMISES: I AM THE LIGHT OF THE WORLD

> *Then Jesus spoke to them again, saying, "I am the light of the world. He who follows Me shall not walk in darkness, but have the light of life."*
> *The Pharisees therefore said to Him, "You bear witness of Yourself; Your witness is not true."* (John 8:12-13)

Jesus is a light unto our path and the light in our lives. He refers to Himself as the **Light of the world** following the testing of the Pharisees when they brought Him the woman caught in the act of adultery. The question was why He brought this up. If we look back at the occurrence, then we see the purpose in the statement. The Pharisees were trying to entrap Jesus with His claims and His knowledge of scripture. Jesus then turned the tables on the Pharisees when He asked if anyone was present without sin in their life. He knew all their sins. He is the one who brings to light and convicts those with sin of their sin. Therefore, all their hearts were convicted, and He confirmed it when He said to them that He is the light of the world. But the light is also the bringer of the life in the one who repents and believes in Him. Even though they all acknowledged their sins and threw down the stones, they were not completely convinced of who He claimed to be because said that He could not bear witness to Himself.

> *In Him was life, and the life was the light of men. And the light shines in the darkness, and the darkness did not comprehend it.*
> *There was a man sent from God, whose name was John. This man came for a witness, to bear witness of the Light, that all through him might believe. He was not that Light, but was sent to bear witness of that Light. That was the true Light which gives light to every man coming into the world.* **(John 1:4-9)**

The Light of the world had to be given prominence in the world because He was the One who gave life. John the Baptist was sent to bear witness to the Light. Even though John was sent from God, he was not the Light. The Light had two functions. First, the Light came to give life where there was no life in your life. Second, the Light was given by God to overcome the darkness in the world and the life of the individual who believes. Those who receive the Light has life. The ones who reject the Light and embrace the darkness will not see the eternal life that awaits those who believe. Jesus is that life and in Him is eternal life. Apart from Him is eternal darkness and death. The belief of the leaders of the Temple were divided. The Pharisees believed in the resurrection and eternal life with God. But the Sadducees did not believe in the resurrection. This was a grim outlook on eternity for leaders in the congregation of the Israelites. This was confusing for the people as well as to the understanding of life and death.

When Jesus made claims to be the Light of the world, this meant to the rulers of the religious establishment that He was the One who gave life. This is the reason the Pharisees said to Him that He was bearing witness to Himself. Only God Himself could make this claim. This claim by Jesus in chapter eight was a bold and true statement as to Jesus' deity. John the Apostle wanted the readers of this gospel to understand the true nature of who Jesus was in relation to God the Father. His deity was always in question among the Pharisees and the other rulers of the Temple. Jesus was a threat to their way of life.

THE PROMISES: I AM THE DOOR

> *Then Jesus said to them again, "Most assuredly, I say to you, I am the door of the sheep. All who ever came before Me are thieves and robbers, but the sheep did not hear them. I am the door. If anyone enters by Me, he will be saved, and will go in and out and find pasture. The thief does not come except to steal, and to kill, and to destroy. I have come that they may have life, and that they may have it more abundantly."* **(John 10:7-10)**

Jesus sought to bring understanding to the disciples whom He mentored. This was evident in the way that He taught. He taught those whom the Father in heaven chose for Him as His inner circle more deliberately than those who followed Him within the multitudes. This promise is one that truly is speaking to the inner circle themselves. Why? Because they have been with Him the longest time, He is becoming more personal in His speech when speaking about the ones around Him. I believe it is a two-fold understanding that He is trying to convey to His disciples. First, the more obvious one, He is showing them that there is no other way except through Him. Second, one day they will have a crucial decision make in the life and He is making them aware of the thief who is out to destroy them in any way possible. The adversary will deceive even the elite from among them, Judas Iscariot and even Peter for a season. They both betrayed Jesus but only Peter sought forgiveness. Jesus gives forgiveness to those who truly seek it with all their heart.

A door must be open by someone for someone to enter. Jesus is the **Door**, so He is the guardian of your soul and your life. Along with this, Jesus is the protector. He is the protector and tender of the sheep and they know His voice. Those outside of the ones who seek and know Him do not hear Him and so they will not heed to His call. But those heed the call and hear His voice will do what He asks of them and are faithful to enter in through the door and not over the fence like the wolves. Those who truly go through Him to the Father will have life and have more abundantly. The problem with the way the church and just basic humanity today functions is out an instantaneous mentality. Most of the time we will not wait to be call to a task. Christians today tend to go in with guns blazing and then when things wrong beg for forgiveness. Doing this saying their hearts were in the right place. But, is their hearts in the right place? If that were the case, then they would have prayed and waited for the Lord and His guidance and things would have been good. Jesus is saying that we must listen to His voice and enter through Him because He is the only way.

THE PROMISES: I AM THE GOOD SHEPHERD

> *I am the good shepherd. The good shepherd gives His life for the sheep. But a hireling, he who is not the shepherd, one who does not own the sheep, sees the wolf coming and leaves the sheep and flees; and the wolf catches the sheep and scatters them. The hireling flees because he is a hireling and does not care about the sheep."* **(John 10:11-13)**

Jesus compared Himself to the ***"good shepherd"***. This is very basic analogy for Him to explain His deity to His disciples. The shepherd and the relationship he has with his sheep is one of the more accurate depictions that show the relationship between Him and those who truly love Him and do His commands without any hesitation. He also adds for emphasis the idea of a hireling. This is like a helper who is not the shepherd and therefore is not invested in the safety and wellbeing of the sheep. In fact, this hireling, when hard times come or wolves come to threaten the flock, he will flee because he is a hireling and he does not care for the sheep. The sheep are not his and so he will abandon the sheep when they need him the most.

The Battle for Eternity

> *"I am the good shepherd; and I know My sheep, and am known by My own. As the Father knows Me, even so I know the Father; and I lay down My life for the sheep. And other sheep I have which are not of this fold; them also I must bring, and they will hear My voice; and there will be one flock and one shepherd."* (John 10:14-16)

The good shepherd will lay down his life for the sheep. The sheep know the voice of the shepherd and will listen to him and obey. The interesting part about this passage is that Jesus goes further by saying that even those sheep of His from other folds He must bring together because they also hear His voice and obey. Then He says that there will be one flock and one shepherd.

THE PROMISES: I AM THE RESURRECTION AND THE LIFE

> *Jesus said to her, "Your brother will rise again."*
> *Martha said to Him, "I know that he will rise again in the resurrection at the last day."*
> *Jesus said to her, "I am the resurrection and the life. He who believes in Me, though he may die, he shall live. And whoever lives and believes in Me shall never die. Do you believe this?"*
> *She said to Him, "Yes, Lord, I believe that You are the Christ, the Son of God, who is to come into the world."* (John 11:23-27)

The core of the belief in Christ as our Savior, there is the resurrection. When Jesus was speaking to Martha concerning her brother Lazarus, she was trying to point out that Lazarus had been dead and in the tomb for four days. Jesus knew this but reassured her of the power of God given Him. He said that I AM the *"resurrection"* and the *"life"*, He was telling her that He was from the beginning in control of life and death. Do we, as believers in Jesus Christ, truly believe that He can do this, and can He do this through us even now?

Martha was confused at Jesus' claim. This is because she did believe in the resurrection on the final judgement day. The purpose of the resurrection of Lazarus from the dead was not as much for Martha's benefit as it was for the glory of God the Father. All who were present at this event were amazed. But Martha made the proclamation to Jesus that she truly believed the Jesus is the Christ, the Son of God, the One whom they have long awaited.

> *Jesus said to her, "Did I not say to you that if you would believe you would see the glory of God?" Then they took away the stone from the place where the dead man was lying. And Jesus lifted up His eyes and said, "Father, I thank You that You have heard Me. And I know that You always hear Me, but because of the people who are standing by I said this, that they may believe that You sent Me." (John 11:40-42)*

Jesus said to them, it seemed with a little frustration, that if they believed, then they would see the glory of God. They did not seem to understand what that meant. Martha nor even Mary believed what this meant. Martha earlier acknowledged Jesus as the Christ and the Son of God. But Martha, when said made that acknowledgement, did not fully understand what she was saying. The purpose of all that transpired was for the glory of God and to the benefit of those around Him. Who was around Him? Martha, Mary, the mourners, friends and family, and the disciples along with other followers. All these people saw a miracle that no one could copy. The resurrection of the dead is one that requires great and unwavering faith in God the Father.

The most noticeable point here is that Jesus, as He prayed aloud, He reminds God as if He were having a conversation with the Father in heaven as the event was unfolding. All power is given to the Son by the Father. The glory is to be given to the Father, even when Jesus did the miracle. This miracle was done in the presence of the many people who were there for the funeral and the time of mourning. This was to help reveal understanding concerning His own future death and resurrection. The resurrection of Lazarus from the death was done to prove the power of God over death and that God through Jesus His Son has conquered death. Lazarus being in the grave was to prove that even though the body was decomposing, nothing is impossible with God. This confirms to the people that God can raise the dead. The question is now, "why did the disciples not believe until they saw Jesus for themselves?" How would we react in a comparable situation?

THE PROMISES: I AM THE WAY, THE TRUTH, AND THE LIFE

> *"Let not your heart be troubled; you believe in God, believe also in Me. In My Father's house are many mansions; if it were not so, I would have told you. I go to prepare a place for you. And if I go and prepare a place for you, I will come again and receive you to Myself; that where I am, there you may be also. And where I go you know, and the way you know."*
>
> *Thomas said to Him, "Lord, we do not know where You are going, and how can we know the way?" Jesus said to him, "I am the way, the truth, and the life. No one comes to the Father except through Me."* (John 14:1-6)

The simplest claim for us to understand is this declaration by Jesus. He is attempting to give His disciples a sense of peace because they are trying to understand that He is going to die. He reassures them that He not only will come back to get them but that He will be preparing a place for them. The signal that they were still understanding or accepting the news of His leaving them is Thomas' question. He was concerned that they did not know where He was going. If did not know where He was going, then how could they find Him. This is a legitimate question. The problem with question was that Jesus had already answered Him when He told them that He would return to them and receive them unto Himself. The answer is that they do know the way to where He is going. Then Jesus gave them the simplest answer.

Jesus said that He is the **Way** to the Father. The only way and there is no other way. In the world today, there are many religions that say they have the way to eternal bliss and life beyond this one. Jesus made the ultimate eternal claim that He is the way. When we look for the answers to eternal life and salvation, we must understand first that there is only one God and that has only one Son and His name is Jesus. The narrow gate that Jesus speaks concerning the path to eternal life is Him. We said previously about Jesus being the Door. The sheep follow the shepherd and the good shepherd is Jesus they will Him through gate or the door. All others are false and will lead you down a path of destruction.

Jesus then said that He is the *"truth"*. Everything that Jesus said or did was first told to Him by the Father. Anything that comes from the Father is truth. Truth is found in God the Father and the Son. Truth is the Word of God and Jesus is the Word that became flesh and dwelt among us full of grace and truth. The truth of God lived among them and they did not even know it. We know the truth is in the Word of God. But just imagine that the Word of God that was with God the Father and was God from the beginning of creation. This was the same one who walked and talked with the multitudes and most of them missed it. People came in masses to be healed or to be fed by this incredible teacher and traveling Rabbi, not realizing who His connection to God the Father. How different would we be in the same situation?

Lastly, Jesus introduced the idea of Him as the *"life"*. Every time Jesus spoke Himself, He said that if they would obey His words and commandments, then they would have life. This does not mean that they would have a plush life now, quite the contrary. Jesus told them on numerous occasions that they would be persecuted for following Him. Therefore, many of the multitudes began to fall away and no longer follow Him. Jesus was referring to the eternal life. Many people in Jesus' day had no understanding of the eternal life. All their teachings were based out of the synagogues and little to no reference to eternal life. If it were in the teachings, it was rooted in the laws and a strict adherence to those laws. Remember that Jesus said He came to fulfill the laws, not to abolish them. When Jesus spoke, He mostly spoke of the eternal life. The Apostle John referenced this in the most popular verse of all time, John 3:16. He says in that verse that eternal life is found only in Jesus Christ. What do you think, do the other religions have a case?

THE PROMISES: I AM THE TRUE VINE

> *"I am the true vine, and My Father is the vinedresser. Every branch in Me that does not bear fruit He takes away; and every branch that bears fruit He prunes, that it may bear more fruit. You are already clean because of the word which I have spoken to you. Abide in Me, and I in you. As the branch cannot bear fruit of itself, unless it abides in the vine, neither can you, unless you abide in Me."* **(John 15:1-4)**

Jesus, in the gospel of John chapter fifteen, said that He is the *"true vine*. When we think of the idea of the vine and its relation to the branches, we must look at our own lives as we serve the Lord. The vine is the only way that the branches receive nutrients to produce fruit. Our purpose as Christians is to produce fruit. We are to produce good fruit. But the interesting point here is that for us to produce fruit, we must be pruned from time to time. God allows situations to come about in our lives to help us mature in our faith. Many times, we question whether God is even there. If we are connected to the vine and we are receiving and obeying His words, then we will produce fruit eternally. Everything Jesus spoke or did was focused toward an eternal goal. So, He said that if we are one with the Son then we will bear much fruit. If we are separated from the vine we cannot produce any fruit and it will be known and revealed in the last day.

> *"I am the vine, you are the branches. He who abides in Me, and I in him, bears much fruit; for without Me you can do nothing. If anyone does not abide in Me, he is cast out as a branch and is withered; and they gather them and throw*

them into the fire, and they are burned. If you abide in Me, and My words abide in you, you will ask what you desire, and it shall be done for you. By this My Father is glorified, that you bear much fruit; so you will be My disciples." (John 15:5-8)

Jesus then reemphasizes the point that He is the vine and we are the branches. But God as the vine grower is the One who will not only prune the branches back. He will be the one who will gather the cuttings of the pruning and throw them into the fire of everlasting torment and suffering. I do not think that there is a choice. The idea of eternal torment and pain in the fires of hell is nothing that appeals to me. What about you? All being said here by Jesus, He gives us a choice. The choice is brought to clarity in the last verse. If you are totally living the life that is in Jesus Christ and through the power of the Holy Spirit, then this will glorify the Father in heaven that you bear much fruit. Jesus said that it only with this will you ever be His disciples. How are we glorifying God the Father?

THE PROMISES: WHAT ROLES DO THESE PROMISES PLAY IN SPIRITUAL WARFARE?

The promises of Jesus Christ in scripture are assurances of His protection. They were confirmation of His love and grace as well as the mercy and grace of God the Father. Are we ready to accept the fact that we are not alone in the battles for eternity? The battle for eternity is constant. The enemy is real, and we must hold on to the promises of Christ. The enemy is being defeated only if we trust Jesus Christ and live in Him as our Savior and Lord. The role that the "I AM" promises of Jesus play are found in where they point us to. This is referring to Jesus as eternal. Jesus was at the beginning of creation and played His part in creation. What makes us think as human beings that we have a better chance of defeating the enemy than Jesus does? Jesus has fought the spiritual since before the fall of humanity. He is winning the fight even today. He even fought and defeated the enemy on is terms as Jesus who was a human resurrected from the grave. He also defeated death and got the keys to hades. So, how can we say that we can fight better than our Lord and Savior. Jesus Christ is the commander in chief of our lives and makes the strategy on the battle lines between good and evil. Will you let Him?

9

THE REWARDS

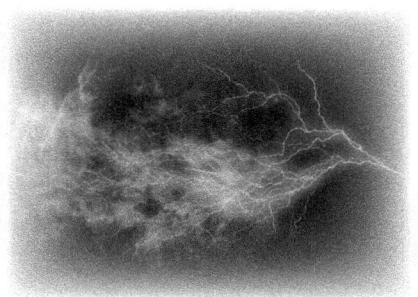

> *The Revelation of Jesus Christ, which God gave Him to show His servants—things which must shortly take place. And He sent and signified it by His angel to His servant John, who bore witness to the word of God, and to the testimony of Jesus Christ, to all things that he saw. Blessed is he who reads and those who hear the words of this prophecy, and keep those things which are written in it; for the time is near.*
> **(Revelation 1:1-3)**

The first great reward that we as Christians have received is salvation through Jesus Christ. This is only the beginning of our daily pursuit of eternity. We must not sit back on our heels and expect the rewards to come rolling in because we deserve them. There is a great measure of grace given to humanity who accept the Lord Jesus as Savior. Living the surrendered life of total obedience brings with it the possibility of death. But, for this person, death is a welcomed reward at the hands of the enemy. Just as the warrior who dies heroically in battle, so it is with the Christian who lives in surrendered obedience to the commands of our Lord.

It is truly evident, as we have seen throughout this study, we are in the battle for our eternal souls. If you believe that there is no evil or even good, then you are sadly mistaken. The book of revelation gives the reader an opportunity to take a bird's eye view of the last years of present existence. Whether you believe that it is actual or allegorical is irrelevant as we consider the big picture of God's eternal plan. There are many people who believe the Bible is a collection of stories and that is all. There are others who believe that the universe, the earth, was creation from a big bang and not a single all powerful omnipresent being. Many, on the one hand, believe in many gods. There are others who do not believe in any gods. What you believe today has the means of placing you in the battle somewhere on the battlefield of life. Now is the time to ask yourself where you stand! What do you believe?

The words in verse three of the beginning verses of the book of Revelation ask three very important questions the enemy does not want you to ask. First, are you reading the scriptures written within these pages? Second, if you are reading it, then are you truly studying, listening, and hearing what is being read from these pages? Lastly, are you receiving and putting into practice the things you read and hear from the pages of this book? Another question concerning this book must do also with the positioning of the book of Revelation within the entirety of the cannon of scripture that is the Bible. This question, I believe, is best answered as the previous sixty-five books and letters of the Bible prepare us for what we are to expect in the book of Revelation. Daily we fight a never-ending fight for our eternal souls against a foe who wants nothing more than to steal, kill, and destroy our souls and defeat God. As we read, hear, and keep the commandments of this book, let us therefore stand and fight in the power and the testimony of our Lord and Savior Jesus Christ. Stand and fight with the faith and knowledge that the victory is sure, and the reward is great. We will investigate in this chapter primarily the rewards that are spelled out in the seven churches in the book of Revelation, providing they repent of their sins as pointed by Jesus. He has won and has defeated the adversary, death, and hell. Amen!

THE REWARDS: SPIRITUAL HUNGER AND THIRST SATISFIED

> *He who has an ear, let him hear what the Spirit says to the churches. To him who overcomes I will give to eat from*

***the tree of life, which is in the midst of the Paradise of God.* (Revelation 2:7)**

The church in Ephesus was first among the seven churches for one reason, their distance from Jesus despite all their good works. The problem with this church was not their works, the works were notable as well as admirable. But it was their motivation. Who did they love? The church was lost at the core of who they were as "Christians." Though they went through the motions and even spoke concerning Christ and stood strong for Him, they lost track of who Jesus was in their lives. The problems that plagued the church in Ephesus were founded in the loss of their first love. They had forgotten where they came from at their conversion. They received Jesus Christ in their lives. Everyone, before they accepted Jesus Christ as Lord and Savior, came from a sinful and fallen state of existence into a wonderful relationship with Christ. These people of the church in Ephesus had forgotten what it truly meant to have a relationship with Jesus Christ as Savior and Lord. They were living Christianity on their own terms. The people in the church had taken the relationship with Jesus, left Him behind, and evolved into a religion of works.

The phrase that is popular with Jesus when He wants us to understand is "He who has an ear, let him hear." Of course, we know that all people have ears and that is not what He is saying. He is reemphasizing for our benefit the earlier statement in chapter one verse three. "He who has an ear" means that those who hear the reading of these words must listen and heed the words and apply them to their lives. He said that they must repent and turn back to their first love and remember from where they had fallen. In doing this, they will become overcomers and will be given fruit from the tree of life to eat that is in the garden of the Paradise of God. Think of our reward to be able to eat of the fruit from the tree of life. Are you or your church found in the dilemma of the church in Ephesus? Do you think there is no way that is possible? We all need to reevaluate our walk with Christ. Believe it or not, neither you nor your church are perfect. We all need direction and correction.

The words of Jesus in the Beatitudes were His first sermon. Jesus said that those who hunger and thirst after His righteousness will be filled. We see this in the ones who hear what He says to the first church. But one must first remember that they humble themselves, repent, live a life likewise before God. The truly humble, repentant, kind person before God will desire with all their heart the righteousness of God. Therefore, they will be filled with the fruit that is eternal life. We will see in all the seven churches the fulfillment of those characteristics of a true disciple of Jesus Christ. Are you satisfied with your walk with Christ? Are you or your church ready to be raptured? Are you or your church ready for the coming battles? Because it is only going to intensify as the time of the end draws closer. What are the rewards of our faithfulness to the Lord? Everlasting life with Jesus Christ and God the Father in the heavenly realms. What is the consequence for not hearing and obeying His call? Removal from the presence of God and eternal damnation. Are we ready?

THE REWARDS: OVERCOMERS WILL NOT TAKE PART IN THE SECOND DEATH

> ***Do not fear any of those things which you are about to suffer. Indeed, the devil is about to throw some of you into prison, that you may be tested, and you will have tribulation ten days. Be faithful until death, and I will give you the crown of life.***
> ***"He who has an ear, let him hear what the Spirit says to the churches. He who overcomes shall not be hurt by the second death."*** **(Revelation 2:10-11)**

The church in Smyrna was one that suffered much persecution at great loss. This was the church that the Apostle John served as Bishop until his arrest and imprisonment on the isle of Patmos. This was a church faithful to the teachings of the Lord. The main

The Battle for Eternity

issue with this church was that they were weakened by the persecution that raged around them. The imprisonment of John was a blow that caused many to stumble, but not fall. Jesus said that He is aware of those who are coming against them. The Jews, who claim to be Jews, but they are not true Jews. He says for them to not listen to what they but to stay strong and faithful to what they believe. Their faithfulness is in the Lord Jesus Christ. The reward for their faithfulness to Lord is that they will not experience or even take part in the second death. Looking ahead at Revelation chapter six, we see under the altar of God at the Throne of God are the martyrs. Those who died because of their faithfulness to the testimony of Jesus Christ. These, I believe, include people like those at Smyrna who will be imprisoned and killed for the testimony of our Lord Jesus Christ. Because of this, they will receive white robes by God. He will avenge their deaths for eternity. If those who persecute the children of God repent of the evil ways and turn to Jesus Christ, then they can escape the second death as well.

Jesus said to His disciples in the beatitudes that you are blessed if you stand strong in the face of persecution. In Matthew chapter five and verse ten, Jesus told them that they will be blessed if you are persecuted for righteousness sake. The reward is the kingdom of heaven. The next verse in Matthew five goes even further. He says that even when you are verbally persecuted for His sake your reward is great if you overcome. The reward in heaven is beyond measure. The beauty of it all is that we are not alone in the fight. As the church in Smyrna were faithful despite great persecution even to the point of imprisoning their leader, we must stand firm in our beliefs and fight regardless the cost. Are you ready?

THE REWARDS: YOU WILL BE GIVEN A NEW NAME

> *He who has an ear, let him hear what the Spirit says to the churches. To him who overcomes I will give some of the hidden manna to eat. And I will give him a white stone, and*

on the stone a new name written which no one knows except him who receives it. **(Revelation 2:17)**

The church in Pergamos was one that compromised gospel for other doctrines. He made a reference to the doctrine of Balaam. This was truly against the teachings of Christ. The things that they were told not to do, they were influenced to and did. Many things that were abominations before the Lord God they did in accordance with the ways of the world. How many churches compromise the teachings found in scripture today, thinking they are outdated or irrelevant for today's society? How many times have they accepted the doctrines of tolerance and acceptance at the cost of the gospel? The church sets the standard that many mainline churches live by today. Jesus said to the church in Pergamos the same statement He spoke to the Ephesus church. "He who has an ear, let him hear." Look in the news today. If there are no indicators in your mind to the failings of the church, then you need to go back to scripture. Do you not understand that worshipping idols in your life is against the teachings of scripture, both Old and New Testaments?

The Ten Commandments found in Exodus chapter twenty starts with the command to not have any other gods before Him. This is to the point. He goes even further with the second commandment. The second is that you shall not make for yourself any graven image of anything in heaven, on the earth, or anything in the earth. These are idols! The problem in the ancient world was that they would worship their gods through graven images of stone or wood. The third is much like the first two. It stated that you shall not take the Name of the Lord God in vain. Now I am sure no one has ever done this one? If you are making for yourselves graven images and worshipping them, then chances are that you are taking the Name of the Lord God in vain. The worshipping of idols many times called for person to offer their children on an altar of fire to a god, or even drink blood to connect to that god. Is it wrong?

The next is sexual immorality. Is this wrong? There were three things that the first Jerusalem Council in Acts chapter fifteen said for the Gentile based churches to do to be followers of Jesus Christ First, they were not to worship idols. This was a problem in the ancient world, especially in that part of the world. Worship Jesus Christ and Him alone and all the teachings must be based out of this belief. Second, they told the churches that their people must abstain from sexual immorality. This means adultery, the "one night stand" culture, sexual covetousness, anyone or anything that you lust after. In fact, Jesus told them that if they even think lustful thoughts about someone, then this is sexual immorality. Lastly, the early church counsel said that they must not drink blood. You are thinking, how could someone do that and not think it was wrong? All of these were problems for the Israelites in certain times of their history. Are we as Christians immune to these abominations? As we look at this point to sexual immorality, yes, it is very wrong in the eyes of the Lord God.

Jesus Christ gave room for repentance in the lives of those in the church at Pergamos. He said that if they did not repent then He would come against them with the sword of the word of His mouth. He informs them that He will come quickly and come against them. The grace given to those who overcome the evils and repent to turn to Him, and His teachings will be mercifulness. The reward is that they will eat of the hidden manna. What does this mean? They will eat on the words that proceed from the mouth of God. The hidden manna is that which is hidden within your heart for eternal nourishment. Next, they will be given a new name that only they know and the one who gave it. When we stand before God the Father and the Son on that faithful judgement day, the name will reflect the glory of our acceptance into the kingdom of God for eternity. Are you ready?

THE REWARDS: YOU WILL BE GIVEN AUTHORITY OVER THE NATIONS

But hold fast what you have till I come. And he who overcomes, and keeps My works until the end, to him I will give power over the nations—'He shall rule them with a rod of iron; They shall be dashed to pieces like the potter's vessels'—as I also have received from My Father; and I will give him the morning star." **(Revelation 2:25-28)**

We know through our understanding of Revelation and the victory that we are assured that those who are overcomers will rule the nations with Him forever and ever. He is telling the church in the city of Thyatira that they must overcome the corruption that is in the church there and repent. The reward for those overcomers will be the right to rule the nations. Not only will they have the right but also the power over those nations. The thought that comes to my mind is based in my observance and understanding of the human condition or the sinful nature. The problem among the people of Thyatira is that of greed. The greed for power as well as the greed of wealth. This takes me back once again to the basics of the beatitudes.

Jesus taught His disciples to first be humble. This is just toward each other in the church, but it was meant toward others as well. As we look at the raw basis of greed, we find at its core pride. The Lord Jesus taught and demonstrated throughout His life that we must first be humble in all our dealings. This does not mean to be doormat. It means just the opposite. In the world, to be humble, repentant, and meek are signs of weakness. But, as a follower and disciple of Jesus Christ, strength is found in these character attributes. These are highly admirable in the eyes of God the Father. The ideas that go against the grain of normal society are those things give us strength through Jesus Christ. The Holy Spirit gives the one who puts all their trusts in Christ a measure of strength and boldness that outshines even the most powerful and wealthiest of all and brings them to their knees in the end. So, know that if God through the power of the Holy Spirit is for us then who can be against us. Remember that as you will rule with a rod of iron and that those who come against will be dashed to pieces like potter's vessels. All the power and wealth in the world cannot keep you from the final judgement.

Jesus told the church at Thyatira that if they overcome, He will give them the morning star. This means they shine bright in the kingdom of heaven. But they must not be seduced by the teachings of those outside world. They must not be allowed within the church to corrupt the teachings of the kingdom and of our Lord Jesus. The teachings are those of tolerance and allowing sexual immorality to grow within the church and not address it. The woman Jezebel, wife of king Ahab of the Northern Kingdom of Israel, was truly evil. Her greatest sin was rooted in her desire for wealth and power by any means possible. The church in Thyatira, and the church today, is called to repent and look only to the Holy Spirit and our Lord and Savior Jesus Christ for empowerment and spiritual wealth. The church in Thyatira was noted for their works, love, service, faith, and patience by the Lord. But the problem was that there was a nasty stain found in Jezebel the prophetess. If this Jezebel is staining the church, then all the good is for nothing. Where are you in your own life? Where is your church?

THE REWARDS: CLOTHED IN WHITE AND CONFESSED BEFORE THE FATHER AND THE ANGELS

> *He who overcomes shall be clothed in white garments, and I will not blot out his name from the Book of Life; but I will confess his name before My Father and before His angels.* **(Revelation 3:5)**

The church in Sardis is one that is struggling to stay alive. How many times have we heard of churches closing their doors for one reason or another? He told to the truth of the gospel to search and find the strengths that you may live again. This is the dead church. There is no life left in this church. The old traditional ways of always doing it this way does not work. As the new generations come into their own ways. They are truly part of the "me" generation. Are you praying for the church to grow physically or spiritually? Jesus is calling us as Christians not to sit back and allow the church die, but we must strengthen those things that remain. The problem today is that very few people are truly committed for the long haul. Most are looking for the specks in their brother's or sister's eye. When they find issue, no matter how small, they live the church to look for greener pastures. We must as Christians be willing to stand and fight for the sake of the gospel of Jesus Christ regardless the cost.

The reward received if we remain faithful to the call of God is the fact and knowledge that our name is written in the Book of Life. We can be with Jesus for ever and ever. The other problem with humanity is that we think we must receive a reward for doing the thing that we are supposed to do. There is another call here, even for a dead church, to at least try to focus and obey God. Allow the Holy Spirit to guide every member of the congregation down the true path of righteousness. The glory of the Lord God is not shown in a dead church. The big question that is raised in the dying church is, how can the church live again? No church ever wants to admit they are failing and unfruitful. Also, especially, no pastor ever wants to admit failure in a congregation. This is the time to realize and wake up as a congregation and realize that we must put Jesus Christ and the Holy Spirit in charge of the ministry and the ministers of the gospel. Revival will come and the church, as well as those people in it, will be reborn into a surrendered life with Christ.

THE REWARDS: FAITHFULNESS OF A FAITHFUL PEOPLE

> *"Behold, I am coming quickly! Hold fast what you have, that no one may take your crown. He who overcomes, I will make him a pillar in the temple of My God, and he shall go out no more. I will write on him the name of My God and the name of the city of My God, the New Jerusalem, which comes down out of heaven from My God. And I will write on him My new name."* **(Revelation 3:11-12)**

The honor and reward of the faithful disciple of Jesus Christ is to become a pillar with the name of God and the name of the New Jerusalem written on it. For those who are looking for status and recognition, the honor and privilege of being a pillar in the temple of God before the Throne of God is most gracious. The church in Philadelphia was one of great love, faith, and longsuffering. They were ones who, like the church at Smyrna, had withstood persecution from the world and from within the fellowship. But they stayed faithful despite the struggles. They did all the Lord Jesus Christ had commanded. They followed the guidance of the Holy Spirit in all things and remained faithful. In their service, they loved everyone as Christ loved them. The beatitudes were lived out as they set a prime example for the other churches of Asia Minor and the rest of the Empire. The fault was not with those faithful in the church but with the Jews, whom Jesus referred to as from the synagogue of Satan. Those who are otherwise known as the Judaizers. With their demands on the gentile believers in Asia Minor, they had caused many churches to faulter in their beliefs and eventually fail. The overcomers of these persecutors of Jesus Christ will have rights in the kingdom of heaven. They will have access and written on them the name of My God, the name of the New City, the Lord Jesus Christ will write upon them His new Name. Are we ready to be the Faithful church?

THE REWARDS: OVERCOMERS WILL SIT ON THE THRONE WITH THE SON OF GOD

> *"Behold, I stand at the door and knock. If anyone hears My voice and opens the door, I will come in to him and dine with him, and he with Me. To him who overcomes I will grant to sit with Me on My throne, as I also overcame and sat down with My Father on His throne."* **(Revelation 3:20-21)**

There had been many sermons preached on the church in Laodicea. This church, along with most churches today, had a problem with commitment to the Lord Jesus. There were many issues that plagued the church in Laodicea but the worst by far was indecisiveness. The other sin that they were exposed as committing is that of pride. They were among the richest areas of the ancient world of the time. But as much as they were may have been rich in material and monetary means, they were poor in the ways of the Lord Jesus. He exposed them for who they were as wretched, poor, blind, naked, and miserable. These are descriptions that are opposite of their view of themselves. How do we view ourselves as in the presence of a Holy God? This church thought that they had it all together. There was nothing missing nor lacking in their lives and the life of the church. The church growing in the way the world viewed them. But in the eyes of God, they were a putrid, rotten, and wretched stain on the kingdom of God. So much God despised this church lukewarm approach to Him that He wanted to vomit them from His mouth. When the people of God are walking right with Him, it is a sweet flavor and it is a blessing beyond measure. But this church caused the gag reflex of God to kick in. This is bad. How do we measure up to God's senses?

Praise be to God that He is faithful and just! He gives us an opportunity to repent of those things which tend to separate us from the love of God in Christ Jesus. The beauty of the love of our Lord and Savior Jesus Christ is that there waiting for us to repent and turn back to Him. He is knocking at the door of our heart. It is not too late for the church to turn to Him. All we must do is answer the call. He said that if anyone hears His voice and opens the door, then He will come in and dine with them. Also, He said that those who overcome and return to Him will sit with Him on His throne in heaven as He sat on the throne with His Father who is in heaven. What a beautiful opportunity. Are the churches ready to stop riding the fence and chose a side of whom your loyalties stand? Are we ready to truly stand firm with Christ as our King of kings and Lord of lords?

The Rewards: Overcomers will receive Eternal Inheritance

> *And He said to me, "It is done! I am the Alpha and the Omega, the Beginning and the End. I will give of the fountain of the water of life freely to him who thirsts. He who*

***overcomes shall inherit all things, and I will be his God and he shall be My son."* (Revelation 21:6-7)**

We are given at the end of the book of Revelation an incredible view of our final reward if we stand strong and remain faithful. The eternal separation from all things evil because of the New Heaven and New Earth will be without sickness, fear, hate, racism, and prejudice. This is beautiful in the eyes of the Lord Jesus. We are unable to understand the true nature of the new creation of God. We see so many wonders today in nature that the hand of God made. We will then have our everlasting reward and there will be no need for sun or moon because it will be eternal morning and day for God Himself will be their God and we will be His people. So, after all the smoke clears from the wars of heaven and earth between good and evil, there is rest and peace that cannot be measured. This is the reward for all the faithful who truly believe and follow Jesus, the Lamb that was slain and lives, for ever and ever, Amen! Do you truly understand the cost of being a disciple of Jesus Christ? The rewards are great, but it is not an easy road. It is costly, but the rewards far outweigh the costs! To Him be the Glory!

The question you may be asking yourself by this time is "why is he just focusing on those rewards from the book of Revelation?" Well, I believe, those promises of the Old Testament, apart from those fulfilled in the book of Revelation, are fulfilled in Jesus Christ, or immediately following Him. Also, many of the ones mentioned in the New Testament find their fulfillment in the book of Revelation. So, for me, all things will finally find fulfillment in the book of Revelation. Is this a simplistic view of prophesy? It could be. Is it an overly basic view of the Promises and their Rewards and fulfillments? We will soon see. The grandest question that begs an answer on our stance is "are we ready as people of God and as individuals in Christ to be called as the Bride of Christ and stand accountable to Him?" Are you ready for your reward to your faithfulness or the consequence for your lack of faith in Him?

10
VICTORY!

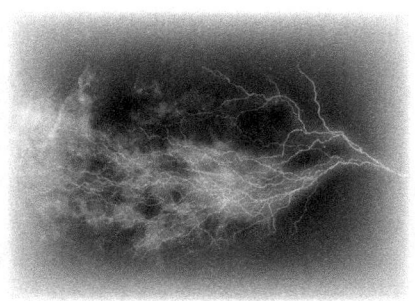

> *So when this corruptible has put on incorruption, and this mortal has put on immortality, then shall be brought to pass the saying that is written: "Death is swallowed up in victory."*
> *"O Death, where is your sting?*
> *O Hades, where is your victory?"*
> *The sting of death is sin, and the strength of sin is the law. But thanks be to God, who gives us the victory through our Lord Jesus Christ.* **(1 Corinthians 15:54-57)**

The Apostle Paul was truly insightful concerning our victory in Christ. The glory of the Lord Jesus Christ is found in His victory over the grave and death itself. God's mercy and grace is endless in our lives. When facing the enemy, whether the enemy within or the enemy outside of ourselves, we must stand firm in the fact that our victory is set in Christ Jesus. The beauty of the life as a Christian is that death and the grave have no hold on us if we abide in the Lord Jesus Christ and He in us. This body that we reside in is only temporary. The weakness and corruption we experience now will be incorruptible and every tear will be wiped away. No pain in our bodies, Halleluiah!

The great misunderstanding of the many Christians today is that we will as Christians experience that perfect life along with health and wealth today. If we do not experience this euphoria in life, then we must be sinful and need to repent of our sinful ways. This is the opposite of the truth. In this present life, we are not perfect. If we follow Jesus Christ and love Him as our savior and

Lord, then we will follow Him because that is our desire. When you look at an army that is prepared for war, you do not look to your families as to the best strategy to conquer the enemy and bring about victory. You look to the leaders who are experienced in the best strategy to set up the missions for victory. If you are looking to be the victor in this spiritual war for the souls of humanity, then you will look to the One who has defeated the enemy and knows His every move, Jesus Christ the Lord and Commander of the all the Hosts of Heaven. There is no better person to lead you in your struggles of life.

OUR VICTORY: DEATH SWALLOWED UP

> ***He will swallow up death forever,***
> ***And the Lord GOD will wipe away tears from all faces;***
> ***The rebuke of His people***
> ***He will take away from all the earth;***
> ***For the LORD has spoken.* (Isaiah 25:8)**

The Lord God will take away all things that are contrary to His glory. Death is only the beginning of eternity for those who love the Lord Jesus Christ and follow His word and live by His statutes. Even though this scripture from book of Isaiah is speaking to the people of Israel, it speaks loudly to the eternal victory we have in Christ Jesus. These are spoken of regarding the promises of God through Jesus Christ in the book of Revelation. This verse from Isaiah resonates throughout the scriptures both Old and New Testaments, but especially in the New Testament. When Jesus died on the cross and was buried, He took the keys to death and hell, so now He has control over both. Death in the final judgement will be judged and cast into the lake of fire and brimstone reserved for the devil and his angels. We want to look to the fact we have conquered death and will go into the heavens with our Lord. Death is no longer a fear for those who truly love the Lord Jesus Christ!

> ***And it will be said in that day:***
> ***"Behold, this is our God;***

*We have waited for Him, and He will save us.
This is the LORD;
We have waited for Him;
We will be glad and rejoice in His salvation."*
(Isaiah 25:9)

The following scripture speaks to the reward from the faithfulness in the victory. We as Christians must not sit down and expect our Christianity grow on our faith in Christ alone. Faith alone is not our salvation or our victory. The understanding of saying "I do" to Jesus at the altar is that you are finished. This makes Jesus out to be a liar. Our desire must be rejoicing in our salvation and act on it. We have waited long enough! Let us now take the shield and the sword and fight in the victory of our Lord and Savior Jesus Christ! Our hope is realized in the victory of the Lamb who was slain and now lives forever and ever! In Him, we find our victory. This verse in Isaiah is showing us even now that as we wait on the Lord, He has called us to the victory. To receive victory in battle you must first go into battle. Follow the Lord Jesus and His commands and victory is ours. The more we stand firm in our beliefs and in our faith, the more He blesses His people. When we follow the call of Him who saved us from our sins through blood, He will lead us to victory over death.

> *"Immediately after the tribulation of those days the sun will be darkened, and the moon will not give its light; the stars will fall from heaven, and the powers of the heavens will be shaken. Then the sign of the Son of Man will appear in heaven, and then all the tribes of the earth will mourn, and they will see the Son of Man coming on the clouds of heaven with power and great glory. And He will send His angels with a great sound of a trumpet, and they will gather together His elect from the four winds, from one end of heaven to the other."*
> **(Matthew 24:29-31)**

The hope that we know in our relationship with Jesus Christ is that we will be gathered up to be with Him when He comes in all His glory. But we must be faithful in all things before we can expect to be included in that number. We will know the victory of the Lord and His coming because of the various signs and wonders in cosmic realms. Our encouragement and strength should be in the fact that we belong to the family of God Almighty. We must be ready and live according to the example and commandments set in place by our Lord and Savior Jesus Christ. The basis of our faith is rooted in the understanding and belief that Jesus, through the Holy Spirit, is our constant companion. He is fighting the fight for our lives with us to the end. He will never leave us or forsake us. In the end, we find our victory through Jesus Christ. The question Christians need to ask themselves is "am I really ready for Jesus to come back?" Are we ready?

OUR VICTORY: DEATH AND THE GRAVE DESTROYED

> *"I will ransom them from the power of the grave;*
> *I will redeem them from death.*
> *O Death, I will be your plagues!*
> *O Grave, I will be your destruction!*
> *Pity is hidden from My eyes."* **(Hosea 13:14)**

Our victory comes from the Lord! It is the powerful hand of Almighty God that is our deliverance from death and the grave. We see this in the revelation of Jesus to John in the Book of revelation. The final judgement is set in place that both death and the grave, once they have given up their dead, will be judged as everyone else. They will then be bound in chains and cast into the lake of fire and brimstone forever and ever. We will see that the victories over death and the grave are true. So why don't we live every moment as if the victory is now and not some later occurrence? Our victory is sure, this we know. Or at least we should know. From this verse is Hosea, the Lord God is going to bring the victory over death and the grave on our behalf. Many Christians, if they believe this, use this as an excuse not to step up and serve. They believe since they said yes to Jesus there is nothing left to do. This is far from the truth.

The sad truth of it all is that most Christians live in a bubble of deception. This is a powerful work of the adversary. Once we acknowledge that the devil is real, and he is hard at work to destroy the testimony of Jesus Christ in the world. Then, I believe that the church will wake up and begin to stand and fight for the Truth of the Gospel. Prayer is our greatest weapon against the fiery attacks. The more we pray the stronger our faith becomes and the more confident our relationship with Christ.

> *So when this corruptible has put on incorruption, and this mortal has put on immortality, then shall be brought to pass the saying that is written: "Death is swallowed up in victory."*
> *"O Death, where is your sting?*
> *O Hades, where is your victory?"*
> *The sting of death is sin, and the strength of sin is the law. But thanks be to God, who gives us the victory through our Lord Jesus Christ.* **(1 Corinthians 15:54-57)**

As Christians, we must not give the victory to the adversary. The churches must reevaluate the condition of the heart and vision of the congregations. Yes, it starts with the pastor and goes through the leadership to those people of the congregation. When Christians look to the pastor an glorify the pastor and not the Lord Jesus, there is a real problem. We cannot have victory is the glory is on the pastor and not Jesus. I am a pastor and have seen this play out in the church that I am pastor and it is not an easy problem to overcome. But thanks be to God that He truly heals. We must claim the victory and run away. When a church is being attacked, the first thing many people do is run. There are a host of reasons and none are truly justified. But the problem is in the fact that they leave to seek a church that if it is being attacked, they can keep their distance. The best thing that churches being attacked need is you there in prayer with them. If you are truly a family of believers or the children of God, you will stay and fight and await the victory. I'll tell my congregation on occasion, "You are family whether you like it or not. You are going to spend eternity with these people you better start getting along with one another." Jesus Christ has the victory not only over death and hades but also over any problems in your church.

Our Victory: Despite all the evils, Christ has the Victory forever!

> *And He said to me, "It is done! I am the Alpha and the Omega, the Beginning and the End. I will give of the fountain of the water of life freely to him who thirsts. He who overcomes shall inherit all things, and I will be his God and he shall be My son. But the cowardly, unbelieving, abominable, murderers, sexually immoral, sorcerers, idolaters, and all liars shall have their part in the lake which burns with fire and brimstone, which is the second death."* **(Revelation 21:6-8)**

The final victory and that those inhabitants of the earth since the creation of the world. Our hope in Jesus Christ has been realized in the new Heaven and the new Earth. The new Jerusalem is the Temple of the Living God and the Lamb. This is the event that we strive our whole Christian life to achieve. Does the world understand this notion of eternal life? No. Our job as Christians and children of the Living God and heirs to the promise of eternal life is to obey the call of God to reach out to those who are lost. We are determined to let someone else do our job. Christians today should be ashamed of themselves. Should we be ashamed? Are we?

The reader of the book of Revelation should glean some understanding. The previous chapters, leading to this wonderful realization of our hope, God gave fallen humanity numerous opportunities to repent and be redeemed. Then, several times, when the opportunity was extended, they refused to repent and turn from their wickedness, but chose to follow their own vices and die in their sins. Many would blame God. We cannot blame God for every adverse event in our lives. Everyone has troubled times and by the same accord they share the same trait, they are human.

The Battle for Eternity

Welcome to life! Why is God always blamed for every bad and evil thing in our lives? On the other hand, why do we feel that we must also blame the devil? As we point the finger in the direction of the most convenient, look at the direction of the other four fingers. We, that is right, *we* are responsible the mess in our life.

For many, the idea of the responsibility being ours for the terrible things in our life is absurd. Do we not make decisions every moment of every day? It is when the important things go wrong that we pin it on the entity or deity of our choice. If we truly have the hope Christ in our hearts and in our lives, then we will quit blaming someone or something else and take responsibility for our actions and our decisions and move forward. Jesus Christ said that He came to give life and to give it abundantly. This does not mean that you store up for yourself riches here on earth. Though there are preachers stand and live by this teaching. Jesus said for us to store up for ourselves treasures in heaven where moth and rust cannot destroy, and thieves cannot steal. Are we as a church laying up our treasures in heaven or putting stock in the idea that the more we have the less likely we are to die? Are you under the impression that you can take it with you? The ancient Egyptians were big on this idea, we see how that turned out for them.

We look at the Christian ideal of eternal life as a "one and done". If that is the way you believe, do not look at the last two chapters of Revelation, because you will truly be disappointed. Why? Because you will not see the new heaven and the new earth or the new Jerusalem. You will be promised a quick ride to the hot pits of the lake of fire and brimstone for eternity. The final judgement will guarantee that ride. Remember, Jesus said that broad is the way that leads to destruction and narrow is the way that leads to eternal life. The one and done theory is just a theory. Are you willing to put it to the test? The beauty of the final two chapters of Revelation is that they are the reward for those who commit their lives solely to the service and the love of God and His Son Jesus Christ, regardless the cost. We need to be preparing the Bride for the Bridegroom! The church must get be prepared for victory or defeat! Where do we stand!

> *Then he said to me, "These words are faithful and true." And the Lord God of the holy prophets sent His angel to show His servants the things which must shortly take place.*
> *"Behold, I am coming quickly! Blessed is he who keeps the words of the prophecy of this book."* **(Revelation 22:6-7)**

Blessed is anyone who truly studies this book of Revelation and meditates on it in their hearts. This scripture is true because we know that the word of God and the words of Jesus are same and true. The beginning of Revelation said the same thing. It said that you are blessed if you read the words of this book. You are also blessed if you are among those who hear the reading of this book and put it to practice in your life. This is our victory against all that is contrary to God and Jesus Christ His Son. He tells us that we must keep the words of this prophecy. This means that must do as Jesus commanded us to do with this prophesy and that is to believe that it is true and live it. Do you believe? If you believe, then are going to live in His marvelous light? Be prepared to stand and fight in His power and might!

Conclusion

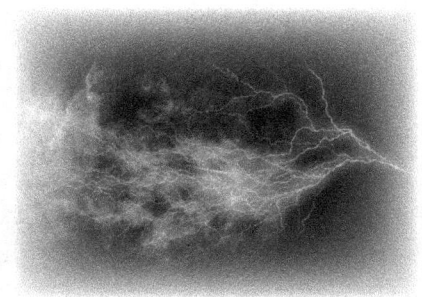

"And behold, I am coming quickly, and My reward is with Me, to give to every one according to his work. I am the Alpha and the Omega, the Beginning and the End, the First and the Last." Blessed are those who do His commandments, that they may have the right to the tree of life, and may enter through the gates into the city. But outside are dogs and sorcerers and sexually immoral and murderers and idolaters, and whoever loves and practices a lie. "I, Jesus, have sent My angel to testify to you these things in the churches. I am the Root and the Offspring of David, the Bright and Morning Star."

And the Spirit and the bride say, "Come!" And let him who hears say, "Come!" And let him who thirsts come. Whoever desires, let him take the water of life freely. **(Revelation 22:12-17)**

The battle of our eternal souls is great and must not keep us from worshipping the One true God and His Son Jesus Christ. We studied the scripture and found that God, in all His infinite love, grace, mercy, and patience endured with immeasurable strength and love for the reconciliation of His most precious creation back to Him. God makes a distinct separation between those who serve and worship Him with all their hearts and those who reject Him as their God. We know now that fear and pride are the two most common means to not being reconciled to the One true God. These are also the primary reasons for people who believe they are Christians not to be accepted into the kingdom of God.

The understanding of spiritual warfare in the life of the believer is one of constant and everlasting battles. These battles have their times of victory and defeat at the hand of the enemy. The final victory has been won by the heavenly hosts and their commander and leader who is the Lord Jesus Christ. The Lamb, the Son of God, who rides into battle clothed in a robe dipped in the eternal blood of victory forever more. The summary of the understanding of the nature of warfare, even in the physical realm, in the end brings with it a high body count. But great thing about those who fight in this eternal war for our souls and stand firm in their faith in the Son of God as the Lamb of God will have eternal life when they are slain. Those unfortunate ones who choose to stand and fight on the side of the enemy and the beast will serve with them in eternal torment in the lake of fire and brimstone when slain in this war. What side are you on? Where will you stand?

THE LORD GOD IS IN CONTROL AND HE IS OUR SHIELD

> *LORD, how they have increased who trouble me!*
> *Many are they who rise up against me.*
> *Many are they who say of me,*
> *"There is no help for him in God." Selah*
> *But You, O LORD, are a shield for me,*
> *My glory and the One who lifts up my head.*
> *I cried to the LORD with my voice,*
> *And He heard me from His holy hill. Selah*
> **(Psalm 3:1-4)**

The study that we have explored concerning spiritual warfare is not one of those who are lacking in faith. This study, I pray, will assist in your search for greater spiritual connection and growth in Jesus Christ through the power of the Holy Spirit. In Psalm 3, David is fleeing from his enemy who happens to be his son Absalom. David, in his weakness, always looked to the Lord God for strength and refuge. The attacks of the enemy are not always from those who are outside of your sphere of influence. The most difficult enemies are the giants found within your own family. Da-

The Battle for Eternity

vid did not want to kill Absalom, his eldest son. Absalom believed that he was to be heir to the throne of Israel. He raised an army to conquer David by surprise and over take the city and the throne. David's generals were responsible for the death of his son and was severely distraught. David, in this wonderful psalm of praise to the Lord, acknowledges that the Lord is his shield and listen when he cries for help in his time of distress.

The war in the spiritual realm is never ending and the Lord is always faithful to those who are faithful to Him. The war for the souls of humanity is fought on your knees. We use terms like stand and fight or stand firm for what you believe. But, in the spiritual wars for the eternal souls of humanity, all the above apply. David is one who stands as an example of the person who rose from rags to riches. He not made it to riches. David in his faithfulness to the Lord rose even beyond the standards of the world to those of the heavenly realm. David not only rose from young shepherd boy to king of all Israel. But the greatest title David achieved was that of "a man after God's own heart." From the things we have learn from this study, we must prepare ourselves to stand and fight on our knees and in the word of God. Also, we must be ready to stand and make account for our testimony even to the steps of the White House and the U.S. Capitol Building. Are you ready to call on the Lord God as our strength and shield?

JESUS GIVES US THE POWER AND AUTHORITY TO DEFEAT THE ENEMY

> *Then He called His twelve disciples together and gave them power and authority over all demons, and to cure diseases. He sent them to preach the kingdom of God and to heal the sick. And He said to them, "Take nothing for the journey, neither staffs nor bag nor bread nor money; and do not have two tunics apiece."* **(Luke 9:1-3)**

The power found within the Holy Spirit and the authority of Jesus Christ the Son of God is all we need to defeat the enemy. It is in His authority to give power and authority to those whom He has sent out. When we are sent out in obedience to the Lord Jesus, it is a step of faith. Many churches, individuals especially, step out with the confidence of the world and not of the leadership and guidance of the Holy Spirit. This passage in the gospel according to Luke chapter nine gives us a clear picture of what He has given us authority over. He gave us power and authority over all demons. That is right, All Demons! Then, Jesus gave us the power and authority to cure diseases. The problem with modern Christianity is that they lack the faith in the Holy Spirit to utilize the power and authority given to us in Christ Jesus. Is it something we fear or are we just lazy?

He said for them to preach the kingdom of God and heal the sick. Jesus tells us to do the same thing today! Many believe that the miracles and everything that Jesus and the Apostles did two thousand years ago happened then and only then. This is a sad assumption and is found in a people of no faith. If Jesus was only speaking to them and not to us, then are we even reading the Bible today? Jesus said that we would do far greater things than He has done for the kingdom. The act of faith that Jesus set for the disciples on their first outreach was one of whole faith.

He told them to take nothing for the journey. Jesus tells us and them that His grace is enough to supply all our needs. He told them not to take anything including money. This was their faith building exercise. He even told them that they would be thrown to the wolves as to slaughter. Can you imagine me as your pastor of your church saying that before you can become a member of the church you must go out and preach? I would have been cast out of the church! But this is the way it should be for the church. I am not saying that I believe a person must be sent out into a world where people hate and revile you and win them for Jesus Christ. But should we do this in our churches? There be would a lot less members. Many members sit around and wait for others to do the work. Jesus empowered them all to go and preach and heal, not one or two of them. He did not even call twenty percent as the

The Battle for Eternity

statistics estimate. He called us all to serve in some sort of capacity. We are the Body of Christ! What if Christ's physical body chose to go in separate directions? How would He have functioned? This may sound crazy and unrealistic, but are we not the Body of Christ and Christ is the Head of the Body? If even half the Body of Christ chooses not to participate, then the other half will suffer. Especially, small churches suffer the most in these situations. Remember, Jesus gives us all power and authority to trample over the serpents and defeat the enemies of this world who stand against the gospel of Jesus Christ. Are you now ready to stand firm and fight for your Lord and Savior Jesus Christ?

WE ARE MORE THAN CONQUERORS IN CHRIST JESUS

> *Who shall separate us from the love of Christ? Shall tribulation, or distress, or persecution, or famine, or nakedness, or peril, or sword? As it is written:*
> *"For Your sake we are killed all day long;*
> *We are accounted as sheep for the slaughter."*
> *Yet in all these things we are more than conquerors through Him who loved us. For I am persuaded that neither death nor life, nor angels nor principalities nor powers, nor things present nor things to come, nor height nor depth, nor any other created thing, shall be able to separate us from the love of God which is in Christ Jesus our Lord.*
> **(Romans 8:35-39)**

The conquerors of this world trained all their lives, and many died in the battle. The war that has been raging against the people and glory of God has been so since before the creation of the universe. The battles have been constant and never ending that have been waged between good and evil. Battles were won and lost for the souls of humanity. In this passage of scripture from Paul's letter to the Romans is the climax of his treatise to the life and battles in the Christian life. We should truly look carefully to the question that Paul is asking. He asks, "who shall separate us from the love of Christ?" The question we ask ourselves is, "what is the love of Christ?" If we must ask this question, then we need to go back and look once again at our salvation. Why? Because our salvation is founded in the love of Christ! The love of Christ is that He came down from His throne to walk, teach, and live among us. The love of Christ is that in doing so He was tortured and died a most gruesome and grotesque means of death. The love of Christ is Him resurrected from the dead and continuing to walk and teach among the people rejected Him. The love of Christ is ascending back to the Father and His throne at His right-hand side and sending the Holy Spirit to continue the work He began. All of which He did not have to do, but He chose to do. This is the love of Christ!

Paul continues when he points to the fact that there are Christians who give their lives every day, for the gospel. Who are we to sit back and reap the benefits and expect the same rewards? If we in fact are conquerors, then we must consider the price that has been paid for our sins and live accordingly. Paul is also saying, whether we know it or not, we enter everyday as sheep to the slaughter. But in this we are more than conquerors through Him who loves us. There must be an understanding that we are servants of Him who gave His life for us. As he said earlier, that even tribulation, distress, persecution, nakedness, famine, peril, or sword cannot separate us from the love of Christ. The big question for us is, are ready to truly serve our Lord and Savior in the love of Christ? Do we really believe and are we ready to live a life in the love of Christ?

WE ARE OVERCOMERS IN FULL OBEDIENCE OF THE COMMANDMENTS OF GOD IN JESUS

> *Whoever believes that Jesus is the Christ is born of God, and everyone who loves Him who begot also loves him who is begotten of Him. By this we know that we love the children of God, when we love God and keep His commandments. For this is the love of God, that we keep His commandments.*

And His commandments are not burdensome. For whatever is born of God overcomes the world. And this is the victory that has overcome the world—our faith. Who is he who overcomes the world, but he who believes that Jesus is the Son of God? **(1 John 5:1-4)**

The love of God is exhibited in us when we love Him and keep His commandments. The commandments of God are given us to live in the love of God. In spiritual warfare, we live in constant readiness every moment of every day for the next battle. In those battles, there rises on occasion, elements of fear. But the love of God casts out fear. So why do we fear? Because we do not understand. Why do we not understand? We do not keep His words and commandments. This is the love of God, according to the Apostle John. The commandments are not burdensome because God is love. The defeat of the enemy is foundational in the love of God and the faith that we have in that love. God's love was given through giving to the death of His Son Jesus Christ. The blood that Jesus shed for you and for me was not just for one moment in time. It was forever ever, Amen! John says that the victory that has overcome the world is our faith.

The faith that is found in the keeping of the commandments of God. This is reflected in the way we worship the Father, Son, and Holy Spirit with a pure heart. When you look back to the beatitudes of Matthew chapter five, you must begin to understand that the big picture of God's plan begins to come clearly into view. Our relationship with the Father, the Son, and the Holy Spirit is in relationship to our belief and faith in the One came, lived, and died that we may have life. How does this make the battle lines clearer for those of us who are in battle with the enemy every day? When you choose the side of the battle with God you are fighting with unlimited resources at your disposal. Satan believes that he has the upper hand even to the end. Do not be deceived by the temporal and limited influences of the enemy for they will be dust in the end. We know that the word of God is the only truth we need, in Jesus

Christ through the power of the Holy Spirit, to overcome and stand victorious in the end. Are we ready to fight and die for the faith?

WE OVERCOME THE POWER OF SATAN WITH THE POWER OF GOD - FOREVER

> *Now when the thousand years have expired, Satan will be released from his prison and will go out to deceive the nations which are in the four corners of the earth, Gog and Magog, to gather them together to battle, whose number is as the sand of the sea. They went up on the breadth of the earth and surrounded the camp of the saints and the beloved city. And fire came down from God out of heaven and devoured them. The devil, who deceived them, was cast into the lake of fire and brimstone where the beast and the false prophet are. And they will be tormented day and night forever and ever.* **(Revelation 20:7-10)**

This is the scene of the last battle of the war after Satan is released from his prison. He gathers all the nations and armies of the earth that remain together to make a last stand against the Lamb and the heavenly hosts. What a glorious sight it will be. This is because the last judgement and verdict is ready to be delivered unto all those who stand with the enemy, the dragon, the beast, and the false prophet and all they stand for in this world. In preparation for this eternal event, God Himself throws down holy fire from heaven and devours them all. God Himself takes care of this final defeat and annihilation of the enemy. It did not say that an angel of the Lord or an angel from heaven did this by the order of God. This was God who cast the fire from heaven! He was saying to Satan, "Enough is enough!!"

The God of all creation also has the power and authority to end it all as well. Do we not take this for granted every day of our lives? Then, we should step back and reevaluate our approach to Christianity. This should be a wake-up call to us and all others who find themselves fighting against God. Because in the end Satan is cast into the lake of fire and brimstone along with his two partners and all those who have rejected Him. I, for one, am not going to partake in the second death and share the same end as all those who decided they know better than the God who created them. This is including Lucifer, Satan himself was created by God and was most trusted by Him. With the Holy Spirit as our guide and Jesus Christ in our hearts, God will give us the victories to become overcomers in life as well as eternal life.

Arm and ready yourselves for the war of your eternal lives!

Are you ready?!

www.ingramcontent.com/pod-product-compliance
Lightning Source LLC
LaVergne TN
LVHW041624070426
835507LV00008B/430